ISBN 978-1-4400-8891-9
PIBN 10276140

1 MONTH OF
FREE
READING

at
www.ForgottenBooks.com

By purchasing this book you are eligible for one month membership to ForgottenBooks.com, giving you unlimited access to our entire collection of over 1,000,000 titles via our web site and mobile apps.

To claim your free month visit:

www.forgottenbooks.com/free276140

English
Français
Deutsche
Italiano
Español
Português

www.forgottenbooks.com

Mythology Photography **Fiction**
Fishing Christianity **Art** Cooking
Essays Buddhism Freemasonry
Medicine **Biology** Music **Ancient
Egypt** Evolution Carpentry Physics
Dance Geology **Mathematics** Fitness
Shakespeare **Folklore** Yoga Marketing
Confidence Immortality Biographies
Poetry **Psychology** Witchcraft
Electronics Chemistry History **Law**
Accounting **Philosophy** Anthropology
Alchemy Drama Quantum Mechanics
Atheism Sexual Health **Ancient History**
Entrepreneurship Languages Sport
Paleontology Needlework Islam
Metaphysics Investment Archaeology
Parenting Statistics Criminology
Motivational

A THEORY OF
URE DESIG

Harmony, Balance, Rhythm

WITH ILLUSTRATIONS AND DIAGRAMS

By DENMAN W. ROSS, Ph. D.

LECTURER ON THE THEORY OF DESIGN IN HARVARD
UNIVERSITY, FELLOW OF THE AMERICAN ACADEMY
OF ARTS AND SCIENCES

BOSTON AND NEW YORK
HOUGHTON, MIFFLIN AND COMPANY

PREFACE

MY purpose in this book is to elucidate, so far as I can, the principles which underlie the practice of drawing and painting as a Fine Art. Art is generally regarded as the expression of feelings and emotions which have no explanation except perhaps in such a word as *inspiration*, which is expletive rather than explanatory. Art is regarded as the one activity of man which has no scientific basis, and the appreciation of Art is said to be a matter of taste in which no two persons can be expected to agree. It is my purpose in this book to show how, in the practice of Art, as in all other practices, we use certain terms and follow certain principles. Being defined and explained, these terms and principles may be known and understood by everybody. They are, so to speak, *the form of the language.*

While an understanding of the terms and principles of Art will not, in itself, enable any one to produce important works, such works are not produced without it. It must be understood, however, that the understanding of terms and principles is not, necessarily, an understanding in words. It may lie in technical processes and in visual images and may never rise, or shall I say fall, to any formulation in words, either spoken or written. The terms and principles of Art have, as a rule, been understood by the artist in the form of technical processes and visual images, not in words. It is in words that they will become generally understood. It is in words that I propose to explain them in this book. I want to bring to definition what, until now, has not been clearly defined or exactly measured. In a sense this book is a contribution to Science rather than to Art. It is a contribution to Science made by a painter, who has used his Art in order to understand his Art, not to produce Works of Art. In a passage of Plato

(Philebus, ¶ 55) Socrates says: "If arithmetic, mensuration, and weighing be taken out of any art, that which remains will not be much." "Not much, certainly," was the reply. The only thing which remains in Art, beyond measurable quantities and qualities, is the personality, the peculiar ability or genius of the artist himself. That, I believe, admits of no explanation. The element of personality is what we mean when we speak of the element of inspiration in a Work of Art. Underlying this element of personality are the terms and principles of the art. In them the artist has found the possibility of expression; in them his inspiration is conveyed to his fellowmen. I propose to explain, not the artist, but the mode of expression which the artist uses. My purpose, in scientific language, is to define, classify, and explain the phenomena of Design. In trying to do that, I have often been at a loss for terms and have been obliged, in certain instances, to use terms with new meanings, meanings which differ, more or less, from those of common usage and from those of writers in other branches of learning. In all such cases I have taken pains to define my terms and to make my meanings perfectly clear. I do not expect any one to read this book who is not willing to allow to my terms the meanings I have given them. Those who are unwilling to accept my definitions will certainly not follow me to my conclusions.

I am giving this book to the Public with great reluctance. Though I have had it in mind for many years and have put no end of thought and work into it, it seems to me inadequate and unsatisfactory. It will hardly be published before I shall discover in it errors both of omission and commission. The book presents a new definition of principles, a new association of ideas. It is inconceivable that this, my first published statement, should be either consistent or complete. It will be a long time, I am sure, before it can be brought to a satisfactory shape. It is simply the best statement that I can make at this time. One reason, perhaps my best reason, for publishing this Theory, before it is completely worked out,

is to bring other students into the investigation. I need their
coöperation, their suggestions, and their criticisms. Without
assistance from others the book would not be as good as it is.
I am indebted to a number of persons for helpful suggestions. I am particularly indebted to three men, who have
been associated with me in my teaching: William Luther
Mowll, Henry Hunt Clark, and Edgar Oscar Parker. Each
of them has had a share in the work. I am indebted to Professor Mowll for very important contributions to the doctrine
of Rhythm, as it is presented in this book, and he has kindly
helped me in the revision of the work for the press. My friend
Dean Briggs has kindly read my proof sheets, and I am indebted to him for many suggestions.

DENMAN W. ROSS.

HARVARD UNIVERSITY,
  February 16, 1907.

CONTENTS

INTRODUCTION   1

POSITIONS IN HARMONY, BALANCE, AND RHYTHM   9

LINES IN HARMONY, BALANCE, AND RHYTHM 37

OUTLINES IN HARMONY, BALANCE, AND RHYTHM 96

TONES AND TONE-RELATIONS 131

SEQUENCES OF VALUES AND COLORS 143

TONE-HARMONY 158

TONE-BALANCE 172

TONE-RHYTHM 182

COMPOSITION. GENERAL RULES 186

THE STUDY OF ORDER IN NATURE AND IN WORKS OF ART . . 190

CONCLUSION 192

PARAGRAPH INDEX 195

CONTENTS

INTRODUCTION

THE MEANING OF DESIGN

1. By Design I mean Order in human feeling and thought and in the many and varied activities by which that feeling or that thought is expressed. By Order I mean, particularly, three things, — Harmony, Balance, and Rhythm. These are the principal modes in which Order is revealed in Nature and, through Design, in Works of Art.

THE ORDER OF HARMONY

2. Whenever two or more impressions or ideas have something in common that is appreciable, they are in harmony, in the measure of what they have in common. The harmony increases as the common element increases; or the common elements. It diminishes in the measure of every difference or contrast. By the Order of Harmony I mean some recurrence or repetition, some correspondence or likeness. The likeness may be in sounds or in sights, in muscular or other sense-impressions. It may lie in sensations, in perceptions, in ideas, in systems of thought.

THE ORDER OF BALANCE

3. By the Order of Balance I mean some equal opposition and consequent equilibrium, as it occurs at some moment of Time or at some point of Space; an equilibrium which induces, for the moment and in its place, a suspension of all change or movement, and causes a pause or a rest. The equilibrium may be one of physical forces (forces of weight or resistance) or forces of will. It may be an equilibrium of sense-impressions or attractions, of interests, of alternative propositions or ideas. It may be the equilibrium of a perfect antithesis. Certain moments of Time, certain points of

Space, are distinguished from others by instances of equilibrium or balance. The balance being lost, in any case, we have at once some movement. If this movement is regular, and marked in its regularity, we get, instead of Balance, Rhythm.

THE ORDER OF RHYTHM

4. By the Order of Rhythm I mean changes of sensation; changes in muscular impressions as we feel them, in sounds as we hear them, in sights as we see them; changes in objects, people, or things as we know them and think of them, changes which induce the feeling or idea of movement, either in the duration of Time or in the extension of Space; provided that the changes take place at regular and marked intervals of time or in regular and marked measures of space. By regular intervals and measures I mean equal or lawfully varying intervals and measures. I do not mean, by Rhythm, changes simply, inducing the sense or idea of movement: I mean, by Rhythm, a regularity of changes in a regularity of measures, with the effect of movement upon our minds.

Rhythms in Time differ from Rhythms in Space, inasmuch as the movement in Time is in one direction, inevitably. It lies in the duration and passing of time, from which nothing escapes. The movement in space, on the contrary, may be in any one of many possible directions. A movement in different directions, particularly in contrary directions, amounts to a negation of movement. In any space-rhythm, therefore, the direction in which the rhythm leads us, the direction in which we follow it, must be unmistakable.

5. Of these three principles of Order, the first and foremost, the most far-reaching and comprehensive, is the principle of Harmony. We have Harmony in all balances, and we have it also in all rhythms. It is, therefore, undesirable to think of the three principles as coördinate. It will be better to think of the principle of Harmony first, and then of two other

principles, those of Balance and of Rhythm, as lying within the range of Harmony but not coextensive with it. We might express the idea in a logical diagram.

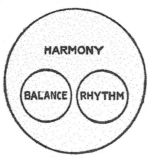

Fig. 1

Within the field of Harmony we have two distinct modes of Order — Balance and Rhythm; but we have Harmony beyond the range of Balance and beyond the range of Rhythm.

In cases where rhythms, corresponding in character and in direction of movement, are set side by side, one on the right, the other on the left, of a vertical axis, so that they balance, one against the other, and the vertical axis of the balance is the line of the movement, we have the union of all three principles. This idea, also, may be expressed in a logical diagram.

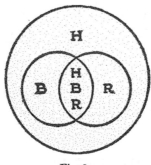

Fig. 2

Examples 'of this union of the three principles of Order will be given farther on.

BEAUTY A SUPREME INSTANCE OF ORDER

6. I refrain from any reference to Beauty as a principle of Design. It is not a principle, but an experience. It is an experience which defies analysis and has no explanation. We distinguish it from all other experiences. It gives us pleasure, perhaps the highest pleasure that we have. At the same time it is idle to talk about it, or to write about it. The less said about it the better. "It is beautiful," you say. Then somebody asks, "Why is it beautiful?" There is no answer to that question. You say it is beautiful because it gives you pleasure: but other things give you pleasure which are not beautiful. Pleasure is, therefore, no criterion of Beauty. What is the pleasure which Beauty gives? It is the pleasure which you have in the sense of Beauty. That is all you can say. You cannot explain either the experience or the kind of pleasure which it gives you.

While I am quite unable to give any definition or explanation of Beauty, I know where to look for it, where I am sure to find it. The Beautiful is revealed, always, so far as I know, in the forms of Order, in the modes of Harmony, of Balance, or of Rhythm. While there are many instances of Harmony, Balance, and Rhythm which are not particularly beautiful, there is, I believe, nothing really beautiful which is not orderly in one or the other, in two, or in all three of these modes. In seeking the Beautiful, therefore, we look for it in instances of Order, in instances of Harmony, Balance, and Rhythm. We shall find it in what may be called supreme instances. This is perhaps our nearest approach to a definition of Beauty: that it is a supreme instance of Order, intuitively felt, instinctively appreciated.

THE ARTS AS DIFFERENT MODES OF EXPRESSION

7. The Arts are different forms or modes of expression: modes of feeling, modes of thought, modes of action. There are many Arts in which different terms of expression, different

materials, different methods are used. **The** principal Arts
are (1) Gymnastics, including Dancing, (2) Music, (3) Speech,
spoken and written, (4) Construction with all kinds of
materials, (5) Sculpture, including Modeling **and** Carving,
(6) Drawing and Painting. These are the principal Arts, but
there are many others, more or less connected with them.
Design comes into all of these Arts, bringing Order, in some
cases Beauty.

THE ART OF DRAWING AND PAINTING

8. The Art which I have studied and practiced, the Art
in which I am giving instruction, is that of Drawing and
Painting.

By the Art of Drawing and Painting I mean expression
in pigment-tones (values, colors, intensities of color) spread
in different measures or quantities and in different shapes:
shapes being differences of character given to a line by its
straightness or curvature, to a spot or area by **its** outline
or contour. By Drawing and Painting I mean, therefore,
expression by lines and spots of paint.

TWO MODES OF DRAWING AND PAINTING

9. There are two modes of Drawing and Painting, the
mode of Pure Design and the mode of Representation.

PURE DESIGN

10. By Pure Design I mean simply Order, that is to say,
Harmony, Balance, and Rhythm, in lines and spots of paint,
in tones, measures, and shapes. Pure Design appeals to
the eye just as absolute Music appeals to the ear. The purpose in Pure Design is to achieve Order in lines and spots
of paint, if possible, the perfection of Order, a supreme
instance of it, the Beautiful: this with no other, no further,
no higher motive; just for the satisfaction, the pleasure, **the**
delight of it. In the practice of Pure Design we aim at Order
and hope for Beauty. Even the motive of giving pleasure to

others lies beyond the proper purpose of Pure Design, though it constantly happens that in pleasing ourselves we give others pleasure.

11. The application of Design in the various Arts and Crafts is well understood and appreciated. We have many instances and examples in the Art of the Past. The possibility of Pure Design, pure Art, followed for the sake of Order and Beauty, with no purpose of service or of utility, is not at all understood or appreciated. I think of Pure Design as I think of Music. Music is the arrangement and composition of sounds for the sake of Order and Beauty, to give pleasure to the ear of the composer. Pure Design is the arrangement and composition of lines and spots of paint for the sake of Order and Beauty, to give pleasure to the eye of the designer. I am prepared to admit, however, that as Music, once created, being appropriate to the occasion when it is performed and to the mood of the listeners, may give pleasure to many persons, so Pure Design, once achieved, being appropriate to the time and the place of exhibition and to the mood of the beholders, may give pleasure to others besides the designer. In that sense, I am willing to allow that Pure Design may be Applied Art, — Art applied in the service of Humanity, its purpose being to bring pleasure into human experience. The underlying motive of it, however, is found not in the service of humanity, but in the ideal of the artist. He aims at Order and hopes for Beauty, as the highest reward of his effort. John Sebastian Bach said of Music: "It is for the glory of God and a pleasant recreation." That is what I mean. The designer, like the musician, seeks first of all to achieve Order and Beauty for the sake of Order and Beauty. That is his religion, — the worship of the Ideal. When the Ideal is realized, the object which has been produced may serve a useful purpose in giving pleasure, and perhaps inspiration, to others.

INTRODUCTION

The principles of Pure Design which are defined and illustrated in this book are the principles which should be followed in all applications of Design in the Arts and Crafts. In such applications, however, the ideals of design are often obscured by the consideration of materials and technical processes on the one hand, and of service or utility on the other. It will be worth while, therefore, for those who wish to bring Design into their work, whatever that is, to study Design in the abstract, Pure Design, so that they may know, before they undertake to use it, what Design is. It is the purpose of this book to explain what it is.

REPRESENTATION

12. Order, which in Pure Design is an end, becomes in Representation a means to an end; the end being the Truth of Representation. In Representation we are no longer dealing, as in Pure Design, with meaningless terms, or, if the terms have meanings, with no regard for them. In Representation we are putting lines and spots of paint together for the sake of their meanings. Design in Representation means Order in the composition or arrangement of meanings. What we aim at is the Truth of Representation in a form of expression which will be simple, clear, reasonable, and consistent, as well as true. The attention must be directed to what is important, away from what is unimportant. Objects, people, and things represented must be brought out and emphasized or suppressed and subordinated, according to the Idea or Truth which the artist wishes to express. The irrelevant must be eliminated. The inconsistent and the incongruous must be avoided. That is what I mean by Design in Representation, the knowledge of Nature and Life presented in a systematic, logical, and orderly way.

REPRESENTATION IN FORMS OF DESIGN

13. It sometimes happens that we have the Truth of Representation in a form of Pure Design or Pure Design com-

bined with Representation. In Poetry we have the meaning of the words in the measures of the verse. So in **Representation** it is sometimes possible to achieve the Truth in forms of Harmony, Balance, and Rhythm. In such cases the appeal is simultaneously to the love of Knowledge and to the sense of Order and of Beauty, so that we have an æsthetic pleasure in the statement of the Truth.

In this book I shall explain what I mean by Drawing and Painting in Pure Design. Later, I hope to write another book on Design in Representation.

DRAWING AND PAINTING IN PURE DESIGN

POSITIONS

14. TAKE a pencil and a piece of paper. With the pencil, on the paper, mark a dot or point.

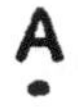

A
.

Fig. 3

By this dot (A) three ideas are expressed: an idea of Tone, the tone of lead in the pencil; an idea of Measure, the extent of the space covered by the dot; and an idea of Shape, the character given to the dot by its outline or contour. The dot is so small that its tone, its measure, and its shape will not be seriously considered. There is another idea, however, which is expressed by the dot or point, — an idea of Position. That is its proper meaning or signification. There is presumably a reason for giving the dot one position rather than another.

POSITIONS DETERMINED BY DIRECTIONS AND DISTANCES

15. Put another dot (B) on your paper, not far from dot "A."

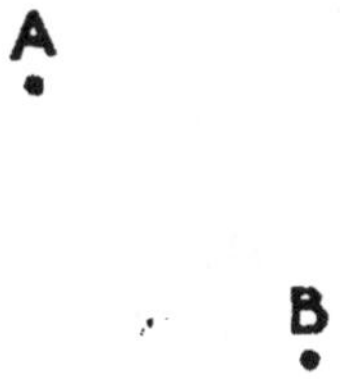

A
.

B
.

Fig. 4

We have now a relation of two positions, — the relation of position "A" to position "B." The relation is one of Directions and of Distances. Proceeding from "A" in a certain direction to a certain distance we reach "B." Proceeding from "B" in a certain direction and to a certain distance we reach "A." Every position means two things; a direction and a distance taken from some point which may be described as the premise-point.

DIRECTIONS

16. Directions may be referred either to the Horizontal or to the Vertical. Referring them to the horizontal, we say of a certain direction, that it is up-to-the-left, or up-to-the-right, or down-to-the-left, or down-to-the-right, a certain number of degrees. It may be thirty (30°), it may be forty-five (45°), it may be sixty (60°), — any number of degrees up to ninety (90°), in which case we say simply that the direction is up or down. Directions on the horizontal may be described by the terms, to the right or to the left.

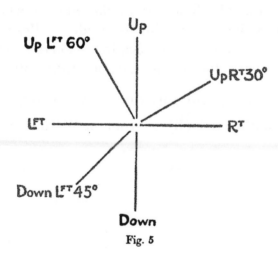

Fig. 5

The method of describing and defining different directions from any point, as a center, is clearly explained by this diagram.

DISTANCES

17. The definition of Distances in any direction is well understood. In defining position "B," in Fig. 4, we say that it is, in a direction from "A," the premise-point, down-to-the-right forty-five degrees (45°), that it is at a distance from "A" of one inch. Distances are always taken from premise-points.

POSITIONS DETERMINED BY TRIANGULATIONS

18. If we mark a third dot, "C," on our paper and wish to define its position, we may give the direction and the distance from "A," or from "B," or, if we prefer, we may follow the principle of Triangulation and give two directions, one from "A" and the other from "B." No distances need be given in that case. The position of "C" will be found at the intersection of the two directions.

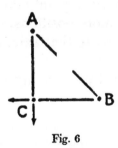

Fig. 6

The principle of Triangulation is illustrated in the above diagram.

INTERVALS

19. We shall have occasion to speak not only of Distances, but of Intervals. They may be defined as intermediate spaces. The spaces between the points "A" and "B," "A" and "C," "B" and "C," in Fig. 6, are Intervals.

SCALE IN RELATIONS OF POSITIONS

20. Given any relation of positions, the scale may be changed by changing the intervals, provided we make no change of directions. That is well understood.

Before proceeding to the considerations which follow, I must ask the reader to refer to the definitions of Harmony, Balance, and Rhythm which I have given in the Introduction.

THE ORDER OF HARMONY

IN POSITIONS: DIRECTIONS, DISTANCES, INTERVALS

21. All Positions lying in the same direction and at the same distance from a given point, taken as a premise-point, are one. There is no such thing, therefore, as a Harmony of Positions. Positions in Harmony are identical positions. Two or more positions may, however, lie in the same direction from or at the same distance from a given point taken as a premise-point. In that case, the two or more positions, having a direction or a distance in common, are, to that extent, in harmony.

22. What do we mean by Harmony of Directions?

Fig. 7

This is an example of Direction-Harmony. All the points or positions lie in one and the same direction from the premise-point "A." The distances from "A" vary. There is no Harmony of Intervals.

Directions being defined by angles of divergence, we may have a Harmony of Directions in the repetition of similar angles of divergence: in other words, when a certain change of direction is repeated.

Fig. 8

In this case the angles of divergence are equal. There is a Harmony, not only in the repetition of a certain angle, but in the correspondence of the intervals.

Fig. 9

This is an example of Harmony produced by the repetition of a certain alternation of directions.

Fig. 10

In this case we have Harmony in the repetition of a certain relation of directions (angles of divergence). In these cases, Fig. 9 and Fig. 10, there is Harmony also, in the repetition of a certain relation of intervals.

23. Two or more positions may lie at the same distance from a given point taken as a premise-point. In that case the positions, having a certain distance in common, are, to that extent, in Harmony.

A
.

•.   •

Fig. 11

This is an example of Distance-Harmony. All the points are
equally distant from the premise-point "A." The directions
vary.

We may have Distance-Harmony, also, in the repetition of
a certain relation of distances.

A
•

Fig. 12

This is an illustration of what I have just described. The
Harmony is of a certain relation of distances repeated.

24. Intervals, that is to say intermediate spaces, are in
Harmony when they have the same measure.

A   •   •   •   •

Fig. 13

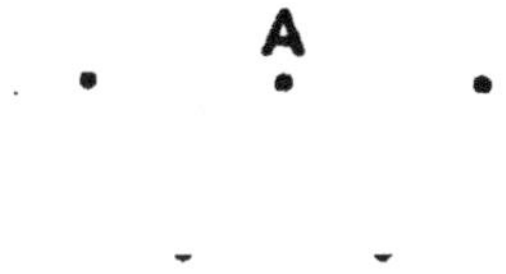

A

Fig. 14

In this case the points are in a group and we have, as in Fig. 11, a Harmony of Distances from the premise-point "A." We have also a Harmony of Intervals, the distances between adjacent points being equal. We have a Harmony of Intervals, not only when the intervals are equal, but when a certain relation of intervals is repeated.

Fig. 15

The repetition of the ratio one-to-three in these intervals is distinctly appreciable. In the repetition we have Harmony, though we have no Harmony in the terms of the ratio itself, that is to say, no Harmony that is appreciable in the sense of vision. The fact that one and three are both multiples of one means that one and three have something in common, but inasmuch as the common divisor, one, cannot be visually appreciated, as such (I feel sure that it cannot), it has no interest or value in Pure Design.

Fig. 16

The relation of intervals is, in this case, the relation of three-one-five. We have Harmony in the repetition of this relation of intervals though there is no Harmony in the relation itself, which is repeated.

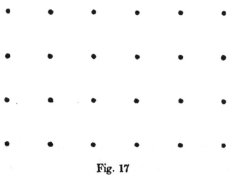

Fig. 17

In this case, also, we have Interval-Harmony, but as the intervals in the vertical and horizontal directions are shorter than the intervals in the diagonal directions, the Harmony is that of a relation of intervals repeated.

25. In moving from point to point in any series of points, it will be found easier to follow the series when the intervals are short than when they are long. In Fig. 17 it is easier to follow the vertical or horizontal series than it is to follow a diagonal series, because in the vertical and horizontal directions the intervals are shorter.

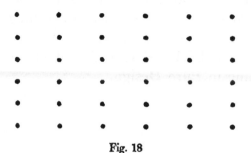

Fig. 18

In this case it is easier to move up or down on the vertical than in any other directions, because the short intervals lie on the vertical. The horizontal intervals are longer, the diagonal intervals longer still.

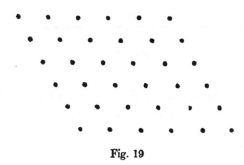

Fig. 19

In this case the series which lies on the diagonal up-left-down-right is the more easily followed. It is possible in this way, by means of shorter intervals, to keep the eye on certain lines. The applications of this principle are very interesting.

26. In each position, as indicated by a point in these arrangements, may be placed a composition of dots, lines, outlines, or areas. The dots indicate positions in which any of the possibilities of design may be developed. They are points from which all things may emerge and become visible.

THE ORDER OF BALANCE

IN POSITIONS: DIRECTIONS, DISTANCES, AND INTERVALS

27. Directions balance when they are opposite.

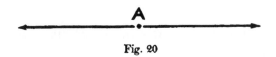

Fig. 20

The opposite directions, right and left, balance on the point from which they are taken.

28. Equal distances in opposite directions balance on the point from which the directions are taken.

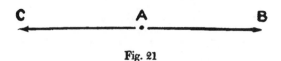

Fig. 21

The equal distances AB and AC, taken in the directions AB and AC respectively, balance on the point "A" from which the directions are taken.

29. Two directions balance when, taken from any point, they diverge at equal angles from any axis, vertical, horizontal, or diagonal.

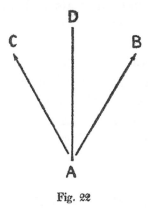

Fig. 22

The directions AB and AC balance on the vertical axis AD from which they diverge equally, that is to say, at equal angles.

30. Equal distances balance in directions which diverge equally from a given axis.

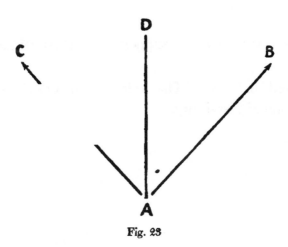

Fig. 23

The equal distances AB and AC balance in the directions AB and AC which diverge equally from the axis AD, making the equal angles CAD and DAB. Both directions and distances balance on the vertical axis AD.

31. The positions B and C in Fig. 23, depending on balancing directions and distances, balance on the same axis. We should feel this balance of the positions A and B on the vertical axis even without any indication of the axis. We have so definite an image of the vertical axis that when it is not drawn we imagine it.

B

C

Fig. 24

In this case the two positions C and B cannot be said to balance, because there is no suggestion, no indication, and no visual image of any axis. It is only the vertical axis which will be imagined when not drawn.

32. Perfect verticality in relations of position suggests

stability and balance. The relation of positions **C–B** in Fig. 24 is one of instability.

Fig. 25

These two positions are felt to balance because they lie in a perfectly vertical relation, which is a relation of stability. Horizontality in relations, of position is also a relation of stability. See Fig. 28, p. 21.

33. All these considerations lead us to the definition of Symmetry. By Symmetry I mean opposite directions or inclinations, opposite and equal distances, opposite positions, and in those positions equal, corresponding, and opposed attractions on a vertical axis. Briefly, Symmetry is right and left balance on a vertical axis. This axis will be imagined when not drawn. In Symmetry we have a balance which is perfectly obvious and instinctively felt by everybody. All other forms of Balance are comparatively obscure. Some of them may be described as occult.

In this case we have a symmetry of positions which means opposite directions, opposite and equal distances, and similar and opposite attractions in those positions. The attractions are black dots corresponding in tone, measure, and shape.

Fig. 27

In this case we have a balance of positions (directions and distances) and attractions in those positions, not only on the vertical axis but on a center. That means Symmetry regarding the vertical axis, Balance regarding the center. If we turn the figure, slightly, from the vertical axis, we shall still have Balance upon a center and axial Balance; but Symmetry, which depends upon the vertical axis, will be lost.

34. The central vertical axis of the whole composition should predominate in symmetrical balances.

Fig. 28

In this case we do not feel the balance of attractions clearly or satisfactorily, because the vertical axis of the whole arrangement does not predominate sufficiently over the six axes of adjacent attractions. It is necessary, in order that symmetrical balance shall be instinctively felt, that the central vertical axis predominate.

• • •   •   • • •   •   • • •

Fig. 29

The central vertical axis is clearly indicated in this case.

•   •   •̣̇   •   •   •   •   •

Fig. 30

Here, also, the central vertical axis is clearly indicated.

35. All relations of position (directions, distances, intervals), as indicated by dots or points, whether orderly or not, being inverted on the vertical axis, give us an obvious symmetrical balance.

• •

Fig. 31

This is a relation of positions to be inverted.

‒

Fig. 32

Here the same relation is repeated, with its inversion to the right on a vertical axis. The result is an obvious symmetrical balance. If this inversion were made on any other than the vertical axis, the result would be Balance but not Symmetry. The balance would still be axial, but the axis, not being vertical, the balance would not be symmetrical.

36. In the case of any unsymmetrical arrangement of dots, the dots become equal attractions in the field of vision, provided they are near enough together to be seen together. To be satisfactorily seen as a single composition or group they ought to lie, all of them, within a visual angle of thirty degrees. We may, within these limits, disregard the fact

that visual attractions lose their force as they are removed from the center of the field of vision. As equal attractions in the field of vision, the dots in any unsymmetrical arrangement may be brought into a balance by weighing the several attractions and indicating what I might call the center of equilibrium. This is best done by means of a symmetrical inclosure or frame. In ascertaining just where the center is, in any case, we depend upon visual sensitiveness or visual feeling, guided by an understanding of the principle of balance: that equal attractions, tensions or pulls, balance at equal distances from a given center, that unequal attractions balance at distances inversely proportional to them. Given certain attractions, to find the center, we weigh the attractions together in the field of vision and observe the position of the center. In simple cases we may be able to prove or disprove our visual feeling by calculations and reasoning. In cases, however, where the attractions vary in their tones, measures, and shapes, and where there are qualities as well as quantities to be considered, calculations and reasoning become difficult if not impossible, and we have to depend upon visual sensitiveness. All balances of positions, as indicated by dots corresponding in tone, measure, and shape, are balances of equal attractions, and the calculation to find the center is a very simple one.

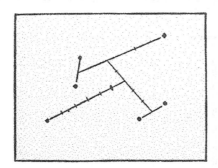

Fig. 33

Here, for example, the several attractions, corresponding and

equal, lie well within the field of vision. The method followed to balance them is that which I have just described. ·
The center of equilibrium was found and then indicated by a
symmetrical framing. Move the frame up or down, right or
left, and the center of the frame and the center of the attractions within it will no longer coincide, and the balance will be
lost. We might say of this arrangement that it is a Harmony
of Positions due to the coincidence of two centers, the center
of the attractions and the center of the framing.

37. It will be observed that the force of the symmetrical
inclosure should be sufficient to overpower any suggestion of
movement which may lie in the attractions inclosed by it.

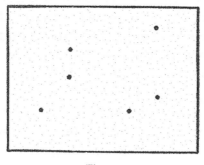

Fig. 34

In this case the dots and the inclosure are about **equally**
attractive.

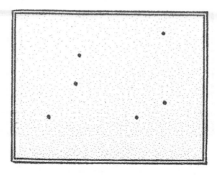

Fig. 35

In this case the force of attractions in the symmetrical outline is sufficient to overpower any suggestion of instability and
movement which may lie in the attractions inclosed by it.

There is another form of Balance, the Balance of Inclinations, but I will defer its consideration until I can illustrate
the idea by lines.

THE ORDER OF RHYTHM

IN POSITIONS: DIRECTIONS, DISTANCES, INTERVALS

38. In any unsymmetrical relation of positions (directions,
distances, intervals), in which the balance-center is not clearly
and sufficiently indicated, there is a suggestion of movement.
The eye, not being held by any balance, readily follows this
suggestion.

Fig. 36

In this case we feel that the group of dots is unbalanced in
character and unstable in its position or attitude. It is easy,
inevitable indeed, to imagine the group falling away to the
right. This is due, no doubt, to the visual habit of imagining
a base-line when it is not drawn. Our judgments are constantly made with reference to the imagined standards of
verticality and horizontality. We seem to be provided with a
plumb-line and a level without being conscious of the fact.

Fig. 37

In this case there is a suggestion of falling down to the left due to the feeling of instability. A symmetrical framing holding the eye at the center of equilibrium would prevent the feeling of movement, provided the framing were sufficiently strong in its attractions. In the examples I have given (Fig. 36 and Fig. 37) we have movement, but no Rhythm.

39. There is another type of movement which we must consider,—the type of movement which is caused by a gradual crowding together of attractions.

•

Fig. 38

There is nothing in this series of dots but the harmony of corresponding attractions and intervals repeated in a harmony of direction. If, instead of the repetition of equal intervals, we had a regular progression of intervals, either arithmetical or geometrical, we should feel a movement in the direction of diminishing intervals.

Fig. 39

In the above example the changes of interval are those of an arithmetical progression.

Fig. 40

In Fig. 40 the changes of interval are those of a geometrical progression. The movement to the left through these sequences is, no doubt, somewhat checked or prevented by the habit of reading to the right.

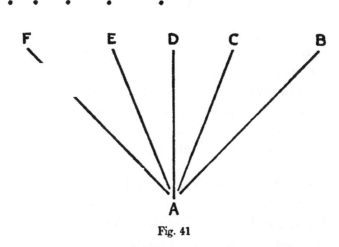

Fig. 41

The angle FAB is the angle of vision within which the sequence is observed. At the end F of the sequence there is a greater number of attractions in a given angle of vision than at the end B, so the eye is drawn towards the left. The pull on the eye is greater at the end F because of the greater number and the crowding together of attractions. In the examples just given (Figs. 39, 40), we have not only movements in certain directions, but movements in regular and marked measures. The movements are, therefore, rhythmical, according to the definition I have given of Rhythm.

40. It is evident that any relation of positions, balanced or unbalanced, may be substituted for the single dots or points in the figures just given. Such substitutions have the following possibilities.

41. First. When the points lie in a series, at equal intervals, the substitution of a symmetrical group of positions at each point gives no Rhythm, only Harmony.

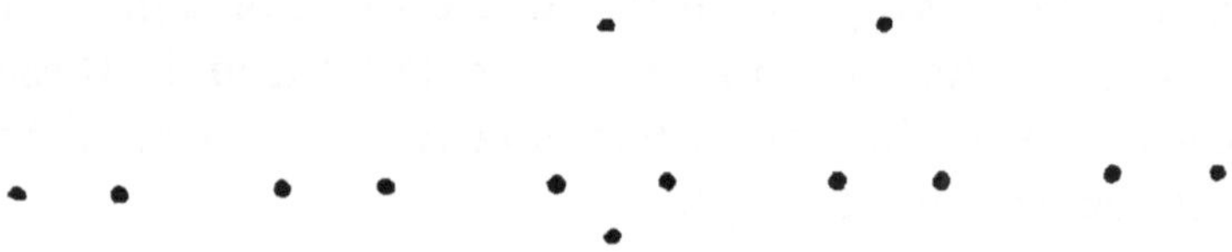

Fig. 42

There is no movement in this series of repetitions. There is consequently no Rhythm. Disregarding the habit of reading to the right, which induces the eye to move in that direction, it is as easy to move toward the left as toward the right. It requires more than repetitions at equal intervals to produce the feeling of Rhythm. There must be movement, and the movement must have a definite direction.

42. Second. The substitution at each point of a symmetrical group at equal intervals, as before, but with a progressive change of scale, will give us Rhythm. The movement will be due to the gradual crowding together of attractions at one end of the series.

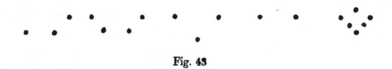

Fig. 43

In this case we have the repetition of a symmetrical rela_tion of positions at equal intervals with a gradation of scale in the repetitions. The result is a Rhythm, in which the movement is from left to right, owing to the greater crowding together of attractions at the right end of the series. The feeling of Rhythm is no doubt somewhat enhanced by our habit of reading to the right, which facilitates the movement of the eye in that direction.

43. Third. The substitution of an unstable group at each point of the sequence, the repetitions being at equal intervals,

gives us a Rhythm, due simply to the movement of the group itself, which is unstable.

Fig. 44

Taking the relation of positions given in Fig. 36 and repeating it at equal intervals, it will be observed that the falling-to-the-right movement, which is the result of instability, is conveyed to the whole series of repetitions. To make it perfectly clear that the movement of this Rhythm is due to the suggestion of movement in the relation of positions which is repeated, I will ask the reader to compare it with the repetition of a symmetrical group in Fig. 42. There is no movement in that case, therefore no Rhythm.

44. Fourth. The movement in Fig. 44 may be increased by a diminution of scale and consequent crowding together of the dots, provided the movement of the groups and the crowding together have the same direction.

Fig. 45

In this case, as I have said, the movement of Fig. 44 is enforced by the presence of another element of movement, that of a gradation of scale and consequent crowding together in the groups. The two movements have the same direction. The movement of the crowding is not so strong as that which is caused by the instability of the group itself.

45. Fifth. A symmetrical relation of positions, being repeated in a series with gradually diminishing intervals between the repeats, will give us a feeling of rhythmic movement. It will be due to a gradual increase in the number of attractions as the eye passes from one angle of vision to another. See Fig. 41. The Rhythm will, no doubt, be somewhat retarded by the sense of successive axes of symmetry.

Fig. 46

In this case a symmetrical group is repeated in a progression of measures. The movement is toward the greater number of attractions at the right end of the series. This increase in the number of attractions is due simply to diminishing intervals in that direction. The eye moves through a series of angles toward the angle which contains the greatest number of attractions. The reader can hardly fail to feel the successive axes of symmetry as a retarding element in this Rhythm.

46. Sixth. Symmetrical relations of position may be repeated in progressions of scale and of intervals. In that case we get two movements, one caused by a gradual increase in the number of attractions in successive angles of vision, the other being due to a gradual crowding together and convergence of attractions in the same series of angles.

Fig. 47

Comparing this Rhythm with the Rhythm of Fig. 43, the

reader will appreciate the force of a diminution of scale in connection with a diminution of intervals.

47. Seventh. Unstable groups may be repeated in progressions of intervals, in which case the movement in the group is conveyed to the whole series, in which there will be, also, the movement of a gradual increase of attractions from one angle of vision to another. In all such cases contrary motion should be avoided if the object is Rhythm. The several movements should have a harmony of direction.

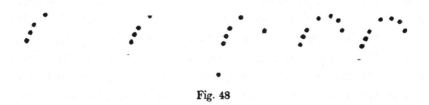

Fig. 48

In this case the movement in the group is felt throughout the series, and the force of the movement is enhanced by the force of a gradual increase of attractions from one visual angle to another, in the same direction, to the right. By reversing the direction of increasing attractions and so getting the two movements into contrary motion, the feeling of rhythm would be much diminished. Such contrary motions are unsatisfactory unless Balance can be achieved. In that case all sense of movement and of rhythm disappears.

48. Eighth. Unstable groups may be repeated, not only in a gradation of intervals, but in a gradation of scale, in which case we have a combination of three causes of movement: lack of stability in the group repeated, a gradual increase in the number of attractions in the sequence of visual angles, and a crowding or convergence of the attractions. Rhythms of this type will not be satisfactory unless the three movements have the same direction.

Fig. 49

Here we have the repetition of an unstable group of attractions in a progression of scale and also of intervals. The arrangement gives us three elements of movement, all in the same direction.

49. Two or even more of such rhythms as I have described may be combined in one compound rhythm, in which the eye will follow two or more distinct movements at the same time. It is important in all compound rhythms that there should be no opposition or conflict of movements, unless of course the object is to achieve a balance of contrary movements. Corresponding rhythms in contrary motion balance one another. If one of the movements is to the right, the other to the left, the balance will be symmetrical.

ATTITUDES

RELATIONS OF POSITION IN DIFFERENT ATTITUDES

50. Given any relation of positions (directions, distances, intervals), it may be turned upon a center and so made to take an indefinite number and variety of attitudes. It may be inverted and the inversion may be turned upon a center, producing another series of attitudes. Except in cases of axial balance, the attitudes of the second series will be different from those of the first.

Fig. 50

In this case the relation of positions being turned upon a center changes its attitude, while the positions within the group remain relatively unchanged. There is no change of shape.

Fig. 51

In this case the same group has been inverted, and a second series of attitudes is shown, differing from the first series.

Fig. 52

In this case, however, which is a case of axial balance, the inversion of the group and the turning of the inversion on a center gives no additional attitudes.

51. Among all possible attitudes there are four which are principal or fundamental, which we may distinguish as follows:—

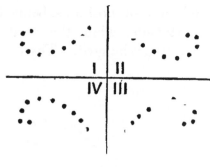

Fig. 53

These principal attitudes are: First, I, the original attitude, whatever it is; second, II, the single inversion of that attitude, to the right on a vertical axis; third, III, the double inversion of the original attitude, first to the right then down; and, fourth, IV, the single inversion of the original position, down across the horizontal axis.

THE ORDER OF HARMONY IN ATTITUDES

52. The repetition of any relation of positions without change of attitude gives us Harmony of Attitudes.

Fig. 54

In this case we have not only a Harmony in the repetition of a certain relation of positions and of intervals, but a Harmony of Attitudes. We have, in the relation of positions repeated, a certain shape. In the repetition of the shape we have Shape-Harmony. In the repetition of the shape in a certain attitude we have a Harmony of Attitudes.

In this case we have lost the Harmony of Attitudes which we had in Fig. 54, but not the Harmony of a certain shape repeated.

53. The possibilities of Harmony in the repetition of any relation of positions in the same attitude has been discussed. A Harmony of Attitudes will occur, also, in the repetition of any relation of attitudes.

Fig. 56

Here we have Harmony in the repetition of a relation of two attitudes of a certain group of positions. The combination of the two attitudes gives us another group of positions and the Harmony lies in the repetition of this group.

THE ORDER OF BALANCE IN ATTITUDES

balance on a vertical axis. All double inversions, the relation
of positions I and III, and II and IV, in Fig. 53, are Attitude-
Balances, not on axes, but on centers.   The balance of these
double inversions is not symmetrical in the sense in which I
use the word symmetry, nor is it axial.   It is central.

THE ORDER OF RHYTHM IN ATTITUDES

55. When movement is suggested by any series of attitudes
and the movement is regulated by equal or regularly progressive intervals, we have a Rhythm of Attitudes.

•

Fig. 57

In this case the changes of attitude suggest a falling movement to the right and down.   In the regular progression of
this movement through marked intervals we have the effect
of Rhythm, in spite of the fact that the relation of positions repeated has axial balance. The intervals in this case
correspond, producing Interval-Harmony. The force of this
Rhythm might be increased if the relation of positions repeated suggested a movement in the same direction. We
should have Rhythm, of course, in the repetition of any such
unstable attitude-rhythms at equal or lawfully varying intervals.

LINES

56. TAKING any dot and drawing it out in any direction, or in a series or sequence of directions, it becomes a line. The line may be drawn in any tone, in any value, color or color-intensity. In order that the line may be seen, the tone of it must differ from the ground-tone upon which it is drawn. The line being distinctly visible, the question of tone need not be raised at this point of our discussion. We will study the line, first, as a line, not as an effect of light.

The line may be drawn long or short, broad or narrow. As the line increases in breadth, however, it becomes an area. We will disregard for the present all consideration of width-measures in the line and confine our attention to the possible changes of direction in it, and to possible changes in its length.

We can draw the line in one direction from beginning to end, in which case it will be straight. If, in drawing the line, we change its direction, we can do this abruptly, in which case the line becomes angular, or we can do it gradually, in which case it becomes curved. Lines may be straight, angular, or curved. They may have two of these characteristics or all three of them. The shapes of lines are of infinite variety.

CHANGES OF DIRECTION IN LINES

Angles

57. Regarding the line which is drawn as a way or path upon which we move and proceed, we must decide, if we change our direction, whether we will turn to the right or to the left, and whether we will turn abruptly or gradually. If we change our direction abruptly we must decide how much

of a change of direction we will make. Is it to be a turn of 30°
or 60° or 90° or 135°? How much of a turn shall it be?

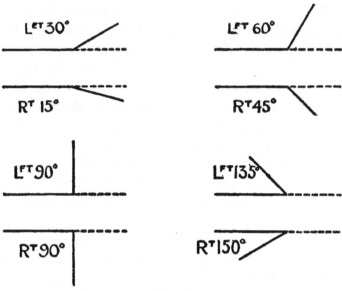

Lᵉᵀ30°   Lꜰᵀ 60°

Rᵀ 15°   Rᵀ45°

Lꜰᵀ90°   Lꜰᵀ135°

Rᵀ90°   Rᵀ150°

Fig. 58

The above illustrations are easy to understand and require
no explanation. An abrupt change of 180° means, of course,
returning upon the line just drawn.

Curves

58. In turning, not abruptly but gradually, changing the
direction at every point, that is to say in making a curve, the
question is, how much of a turn to make in a given distance,
through how many degrees of the circle to turn in one inch
(1″), in half an inch (½″), in two inches (2″).   In estimating
the relation of arcs, as distances, to angles of curvature, the
angles of the arcs, the reader will find it convenient to refer
to what I may call an Arc-Meter. The principle of this
meter is shown in the following diagram: —

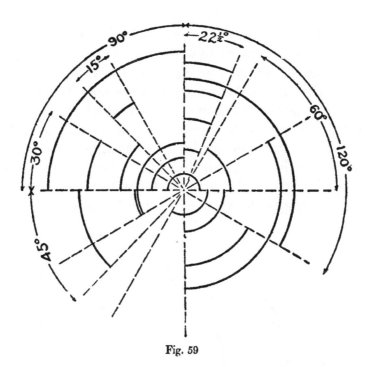

Fig. 59

If we wish to turn 30° in $\frac{1}{2}''$, we take the angle of 30° and look within it for an arc of $\frac{1}{2}''$. The arc of the right length and the right angle being found, it can be drawn free-hand or mechanically, by tracing or by the dividers. Using this meter, we are able to draw any curve or combination of curves, approximately; and we are able to describe and define a line, in its curvatures, so accurately that it can be produced according to the definition. Owing, however, to the difficulty of measuring the length of circular arcs accurately, we may find it simpler to define the circular arc by the length of its radius and the angle through which the radius passes when the arc is drawn.

Fig. 60

Here, for example, is a certain circular arc. It is perhaps best defined and described as the arc of a half inch radius and an angle of ninety degrees, or in writing, more briefly, rad. $\frac{1}{2}''$ 90°. Regarding every curved line either as a circular arc or made up of a series of circular arcs, the curve may be defined and described by naming the arc or arcs of which it is composed, in the order in which they are to be drawn, and the attitude of the curve may be determined by starting from a certain tangent drawn in a certain direction. The direction of the tangent being given, the first arc takes the direction of the tangent, turning to the right of it or to the left.

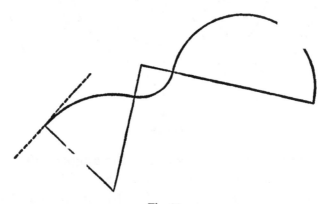

Fig. 61

Here is a curve which is composed of four circular arcs to be drawn in the following order: —

Tangent up right 45°, arc right radius 1″ 60°, arc left radius $\frac{1}{3}''$ 90°, arc right radius $\frac{3}{4}''$ 180°.

Two arcs will often come together at an angle. The definition of the angle must be given in that case. It is, of course, the angle made by tangents of the arcs. Describing the first arc and the direction (right or left so many degrees) which the tangent of the second arc takes from the tangent of the first arc; then describing the second arc and stating whether it turns from its tangent to the right or to the left, we shall be able to describe, not only our curves, but any angles which may occur in them.

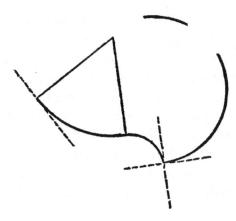

Fig. 62

Here is a curve which, so far as the arcs are concerned, of which it is composed, resembles the curve of Fig. 61; but in this case the third arc makes an angle with the second. That angle has to be defined. Drawing the tangents, it appears to be a right angle. The definition of the line given in Fig. 62 will read as follows: —

Tangent down right 45°, arc left radius 1″ 60°, arc right radius $\frac{1}{3}$″ 90°, tangent left 90°, arc left $\frac{3}{4}$″ 180°.

59. In this way, regarding all curves as circular arcs or composed of circular arcs, we shall be able to define any line we see, or any line which we wish to produce, so far as changes of direction are concerned. For the purposes of this discussion, I shall consider all curves as composed of circular arcs.

There are many curves, of course, which are not circular in character, nor composed, strictly speaking, of circular arcs. The Spirals are in no part circular. Elliptical curves are in no part circular. All curves may, nevertheless, be approximately drawn as compositions of circular arcs. The approximation to curves which are not circular may be easily carried beyond any power of discrimination which we have in the sense of vision. The method of curve-definition, which I have described, though it may not be strictly mathematical, will be found satisfactory for all purposes of Pure Design. It is very important that we should be able to analyze our lines upon a single general principle; to discover whether they are illustrations of Order. We must know whether any given line, being orderly, is orderly in the sense of Harmony, Balance, or Rhythm. It is equally important, if we wish to produce an orderly as distinguished from a disorderly line, that we should have some general principle to follow in doing it, that we should be able to produce forms of Harmony or Balance or Rhythm in a line, if we wish to do so.

DIFFERENCES OF SCALE IN LINES

60. Having drawn a line of a certain shape, either straight or angular or curved, or partly angular, partly curved, we may change the measure of the line, in its length, without changing its shape. That is to say, we may draw the line longer or shorter, keeping all changes of direction, such as they are, in the same positions, relatively. In that way the same shape may be drawn larger or smaller. That is what we mean when we speak of a change of scale or of measure which is not a change of shape.

DIFFERENCES OF ATTRACTION IN LINES

61. A line attracts attention in the measure of the tone-contrast which it makes with the ground-tone upon which it is drawn. It attracts attention, also, according to its length, which is an extension of the tone-contrast. It attracts more attention the longer it is, provided it lies, all of it, well within the field of vision. It attracts attention also in the measure of its concentration.

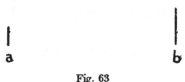

a   b

Fig. 63

Line "a" would attract less attention than it does if the tone-contrast, black on a ground of white paper, were diminished, if the line were gray, not black. In line "b" there is twice the extension of tone-contrast there is in "a." For that reason "b" is more attractive. If, however, "a" were black and "b" were gray, "a" might be more attractive than "b," because of the greater tone-contrast.

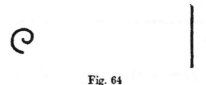

Fig. 64

In this illustration the curved line is more attractive than the straight line because it is more concentrated, therefore more definite. The extent of tone-contrast is the same, the lines being of the same length.

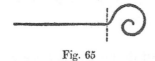

Fig. 65

In this line there is no doubt as to the greater attraction of the twisted end, on account of the greater concentration it exhibits. The extent of tone-contrast is the same at both ends. The force of attraction in the twisted end of the line would be diminished if the twisted end were made gray instead of black. The pull of concentration at one end might, conceivably, be perfectly neutralized by the pull of a greater tone-contrast at the other.

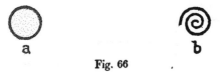

a   b

Fig. 66   .

This might not be the case, however, if the greater extension of tone-contrast in one case were neutralized by an increase of tone-contrast in the other.

62. Harmony of Direction means no change of direction.

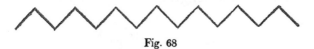

Fig. 67

In this case we have a Harmony of Direction in the line, because it does not change its direction.

63. Harmony of Angles.   We may have Harmony in the repetition of a certain relation of directions, as in an angle.

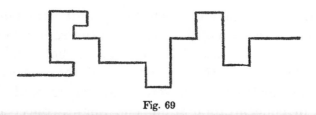

Fig. 68

The angle up **45°** and down **45°** is here repeated seven times.

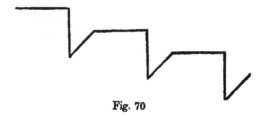

Fig. 69

In this case we have a great many angles in the line, but they are all right angles, so we have a Harmony of Angles.

Fig. 70

In this case we have Harmony in the repetition of a certain relation of angles, that is to say, in the repetition of a certain form of angularity.

64. Equality of lengths or measures between the angles of a line means a Harmony of Measures.

Fig. 71

In this case, for example, we have no Harmony of Angles, but a Harmony of Measures in the legs of the angles, as they are called.

65. We have a Harmony of Curvature in a line when it is composed wholly of arcs of the same radius and the same angle.

Fig. 72

This is a case of Harmony of Curvature. There is no change of direction here, in the sequence of corresponding arcs.

Fig. 73

Here, again, we have a Harmony of Curvature. In this case, however, there is a regular alternation of directions in the sequence of corresponding arcs. In this regular alternation, which is the repetition of a certain relation of directions, there is a Harmony of Directions.

Fig. 74

In this case the changes of direction are abrupt (angular) as well as gradual. There is no regular alternation, but the harmony of corresponding arcs repeated will be appreciated, nevertheless.

66. Arcs produced by the same radius are in harmony to that extent, having the radius in common.

Fig. 75

This is an example of a harmony of arcs produced by radii of the same length. The arcs vary in length.

67. Arcs of the same angle-measure produced by different radii are in Harmony to the extent that they have an angle-measure in common.

Fig. 76

This is an example.

Arcs having the same length but varying in both radius and angle may be felt to be in Measure-Harmony. It is doubtful, however, whether lines of the same length but of very different curvatures will be felt to correspond. If the correspondence of lengths is not felt, visually, it has no interest or value from the point of view of Pure Design.

68. Any line may be continued in a repetition or repetitions of its shape, whatever the shape is, producing what I call a Linear Progression. In the repetitions we have Shape-Harmony.

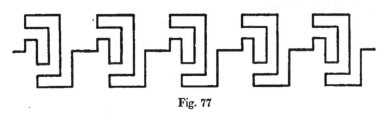

Fig. 77

This is an example of Linear Progression. The character of the progression is determined by the shape-motive which is repeated in it.

69. The repetition of a certain shape-motive in a line is not, necessarily, a repetition in the same measure or scale. A repetition of the same shape in the same measure means Measure and Shape-Harmony in the progression. A repetition ₡of the same shape in different measures means Shape-Harmony without Measure-Harmony.

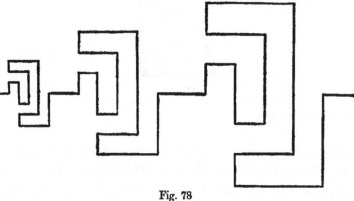

Fig. 78

Here we have the repetition of a certain shape in a line, in a progression of measures.   That gives us Shape-Harmony and a Harmony of Proportions, without Measure-Harmony.

70. In the repetition of a certain shape-motive in the line, the line may change its direction abruptly or gradually, continuously or alternately, producing a Linear Progression with changes of direction.

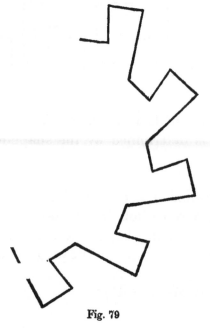

Fig. 79

In Fig. 79 there is a certain change of direction as we pass from one repetition to the next. In the repetition of the same change of direction, of the same angle of divergence, we have Harmony. If the angles of divergence varied we should have no such Harmony, though we might have Harmony in the repetition of a certain relation of divergences. Any repetition of a certain change or changes of direction in a linear progression gives a Harmony of Directions in the progression.

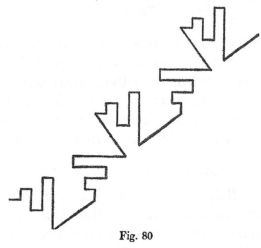

Fig. 80

In this case there is a regular alternation of directions in the repeats. The repeats are drawn first to the right, then up, and the relation of these two directions is then repeated.

71. By inverting the motive of any progression, in single or in double inversion, and repeating the motive together with its inversion, we are able to vary the character of the progression indefinitely.

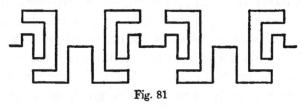

Fig. 81

In this case we have a single inversion of the motive and a

repetition of the motive with its inversion. Compare this progression with the one in Fig. 77, where the same motive is repeated without inversion.

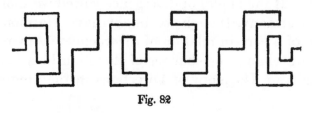

Fig. 82

Here we have the same motive with a double inversion, the motive with its double inversion being repeated. The inversion gives us Shape-Harmony without Harmony of Attitudes. We have Harmony, however, in a repetition of the relation of two attitudes. These double inversions are more interesting from the point of view of Balance than of Harmony.

THE ORDER OF BALANCE IN LINES

72. We have Balance in a line when one half of it is the single or double inversion of the other half; that is, when there is an equal opposition and consequent equilibrium of attractions in the line. When the axis of the inversion is vertical the balance is symmetrical.

<hr>

Fig. 83

There is Balance in this line because half of it is the single inversion of the other half. The balance is symmetrical because the axis is vertical. The balance, although symmetrical, is not likely to be appreciated, however, because the eye is sure to move along a line upon which there is no better reason for not moving than is found in slight terminal contrasts. The eye is not held at the center when there is nothing to hold the eye on the center. Mark the center in any way and the eye will go to it at once. A mark or accent may be put at the center, or accents, corresponding and equal, may

be put at equal distances from the center in opposite directions. The eye will then be held at the center by the force
of equal and opposite attractions.

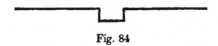

Fig. 84

In this case the eye is held at the balance-center of the line
by a change of character at that point.

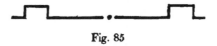

Fig. 85

In this case the changes of character are at equal distances,
in opposite directions, from the center. The center is marked
by a break. The axis being vertical, the balance is a symmetrical one.

73. The appreciation of Balance in a line depends very
much upon the attitude in which it is drawn.

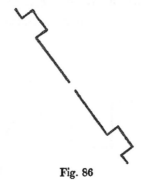

Fig. 86

In this case the balance in the line itself is just as good as
it is in Fig. 85; but the axis of the balance being diagonal, the
balance is less distinctly felt. The balance is unsatisfactory
because the attitude of the line is one which suggests a falling
down to the left. It is the instability of the line which is
felt, more than the balance in it.

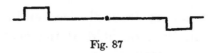

Fig. 87

In this case of double inversion, also, we have balance. The balance is more distinctly felt than it was in Fig. 86. The attitude is one of stability. This balance is neither axial nor symmetrical, but central.

74. A line balances, in a sense, when its inclinations are balanced.

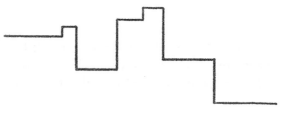

Fig. 88

This line may be said to be in balance, as it has no inclinations, either to the right or to the left, to suggest instability. The verticals and the horizontals, being stable, look after themselves perfectly well.

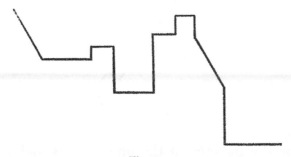

Fig. 89

This line has two unbalanced inclinations to the left. It is, therefore, less satisfactory than the line in Fig. 88, from the point of view of Balance.

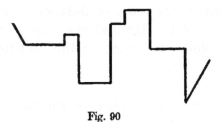

Fig. 90

The two inclinations in this line counteract one another. One inclination toward the left is balanced by a corresponding inclination toward the right.

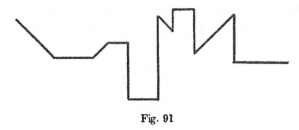

Fig. 91

In this case, also, there is no inclination toward the left which is not balanced by a corresponding inclination toward the right.

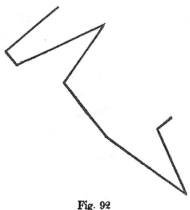

Fig. 92

In this line, which is composed wholly of inclinations to the right or left, every inclination is balanced, and the line is, therefore, orderly in the sense of Balance; more so, certainly, than it would be if the inclinations were not counteracted. This is the problem of balancing the directions or inclinations of a line.

75. A line having no balance or symmetry in itself may become balanced. The line may be regarded as if it were a series of dots close together. The line is then a relation of positions indicated by dots. It is a composition of attractions corresponding and equal. It is only necessary, then, to find what I have called the center of equilibrium, the balance-center of the attractions, and to indicate that center by a symmetrical inclosure. The line will then become balanced.

Fig. 93

Here is a line. To find the center of its attractions it may be considered as if it were a line of dots, like this: —

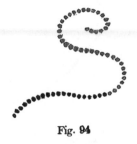

Fig. 94

The principle according to which we find the balance-center is stated on page 23. The balance-center being found, it must be indicated unmistakably. This may be done by means

of any symmetrical inclosure which will draw the eye to the
center and hold it there.

Fig. 95

In this case the balance-center is indicated by a rectangular
inclosure. This rectangle is not, however, in harmony of
character with the line inclosed by it, which is curved.

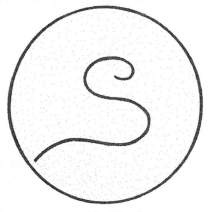

Fig. 96

In this case the balance-center is indicated by a circle, which,
being a curve, is in harmony of character with the inclosed
line, which is also a curve. I shall call this Occult Balance
to distinguish it from the unmistakable Balance of Symmetry
and other comparatively obvious forms of Balance, including
the balance of double inversions. As I have said, on page 24,

the symmetrical framing must be sufficiently attractive to hold the eye steadily at the center, otherwise it does not serve its purpose.

THE ORDER OF RHYTHM IN LINES

76. The eye, not being held on a vertical axis or on a balance-center, readily follows any suggestion of movement.

Fig. 97

In this case there is no intimation of any vertical axis or balance-center. The figure is consequently unstable. There is a sense of movement to the right. This is due, not only to the inclinations to the right, but to the convergences in that direction.

Fig. 98

In this case the movement is unmistakably to the left. In such cases we have movement, but no Rhythm.

77. Rhythm requires, not only movement, but the order of regular and marked intervals.

Fig. 99

In Fig. 99 we have a line, a linear progression, which gives us the feeling of movement, unmistakably. The movement, which in the motive itself is not rhythmical, becomes rhythmical in its repetition at regular, and in this case equal, intervals. The intervals are marked by the repetitions.

78. It is a question of some interest to decide how many repetitions are required in a Rhythm. In answer to this question I should say three as a rule. A single repetition shows us only one interval, and we do not know whether the succeeding intervals are to be equal or progressive, arithmetically progressive or geometrically progressive. The rhythm is not defined until this question is decided, as it will be by two more repetitions. The measures of the rhythm might take the form of a repeated relation of measures; a repetition, for example, of the measures two, seven, four. In that case the relation of the three measures would have to be repeated at least three times before the character of the rhythm could be appreciated.

79. Any contrariety of movement in the motive is extended, of course, to its repetitions.

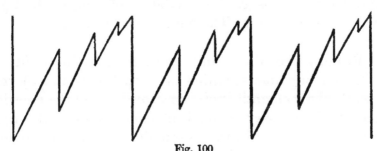

Fig. 100

Fig. 101

In this case, by omitting the long vertical line I have diminished the amount of convergence downward. In that way I have given predominance to the upward movement. Instead of altogether omitting the long vertical line, I might have changed its tone from black to gray. That would cause an approximate instead of complete disappearance. It should be remembered that in all these cases the habit of reading comes in to facilitate the movements to the right. It is easier for the eye to move to the right than in any other direction, other things being equal. The movement back to the beginning of another line, which is of course inevitable in reading, produces comparatively little impression upon us, no more than the turning of the page. The habit of reading to the right happens to be our habit. The habit is not universal.

80. Reading repetitions and alternations to the right, always, I, for a long time, regarded such repetitions and alternations as rhythmical, until Professor Mowll raised the question whether it is necessary to read all alternations to the right when there is nothing in the alternations themselves to suggest a movement in one direction rather than another. Why not read them to the left as well as to the right? We at once decided that the movement in a Rhythm must be determined by the character of the Rhythm itself, not by any habit of reading, or any other habit, on our part. It was in that way that we came to regard repetitions and alternations as illustrations of Harmony rather than of Rhythm. Rhythm comes

into the Harmony of a Repeated Relation when the relation
is one which causes the eye to move in one direction rather
than another, and when the movement is carried on from
repetition to repetition, from measure to measure.

81. The repetition of a motive at equal intervals, when there
is no movement in the motive, gives us no feeling of Rhythm.

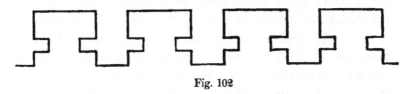

Fig. 102

In this case, for example, we have a repetition in the line of a
certain symmetrical shape. As there is no movement in the
shape repeated, there is no Rhythm in the repetition. There
is nothing to draw the eye in one direction rather than another. The attractions at one end of the line correspond with
the attractions at the other.

82. The feeling of Rhythm may be induced by a regular
diminution of measure or scale in the repetitions of the
motive and in the intervals in which the repetitions take place.

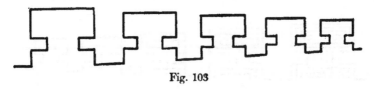

Fig. 103

In this case the shape repeated is still symmetrical, but it is
repeated with a gradual diminution of scale and of intervals,
by which we are given a feeling of rhythmic movement.
The change of scale and of intervals, to induce a sense of
rhythmic motion, must be regular. To be regular the change
must be in the terms of one or the other of the regular progressions; the arithmetical progression, which proceeds by

a certain addition, or the geometrical, which proceeds by a certain multiplication. The question may arise in this case (Fig. 103) whether the movement of the Rhythm is to the right or to the left. I feel, myself, that the movement is to the right. In diminishing the scale of the motive and of the intervals we have, hardly at all, diminished the extent of the tone-contrast in a given angle of vision. See Fig. 41, p. 27, showing the increase of attractions from one visual angle to another. At the same time we come at the right end of the progression to two or more repetitions in the space of one. We have, therefore, established the attraction of a crowding together at the right end of the series. See the passage (p. 43) on the attractiveness of a line. The force of the crowding together of attractions is, I feel, sufficient to cause a movement to the right. It must be remembered, however, that the greater facility of reading to the right is added here to the pull of a greater crowding together of attractions in the same direction, so the movement of the Rhythm in that direction may not be very strong after all. If the direction of any Rhythm is doubtful, the Rhythm itself is doubtful.

83. The feeling of Rhythm may be induced, as I have said, by a gradual increase of the number of attractions from measure to measure, an increase of the extent of tone-contrast.

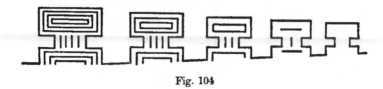

Fig. 104

Increasing the extent of tone-contrast and the number of attractions in the measures of the Rhythm in Fig. 103, we are able to force the eye to follow the series in the direction contrary to the habit of reading, that is to say from right to left.

A decrease in the forces of attraction in connection with a decrease of scale is familiar to us all in the phenomena of

perspective. The gradual disappearance of objects in aerial
perspective does away with the attraction of a greater crowding together of objects in the distance.

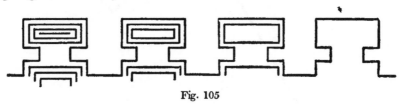

Fig. 105

In this case the diminution of scale has been given up and
there is no longer any crowding together. There is no chance
of this rhythm being read from left to right except by an
effort of the will. The increase of attractions toward the left is
much more than sufficient to counteract the habit of reading.

84. The force of a gradual coming together of attractions,
inducing movement in the direction of such coming together,
is noticeable in spiral shapes.

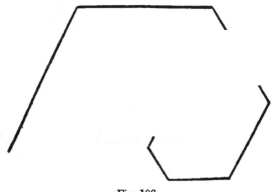

Fig. 106

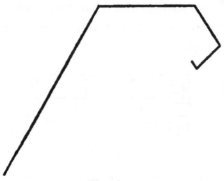

Fig. 107

In this case we have a series of straight lines with a constant change of direction to the right; but in this case the changes of measure in the lines are in the terms of a geometrical progression. The direction is the same, the pull of concentration perhaps stronger.

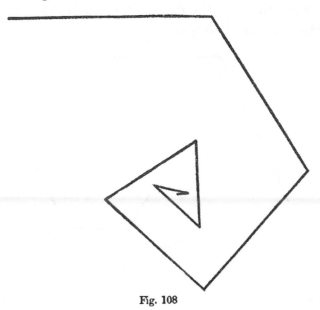

Fig. 108

In this Rhythm there is an arithmetical gradation of meăsures in the changes of direction, both in the length of the legs and in the measure of the angles. The pull of concentration is, in this case, very much increased. It is evident that the legs may vary arithmetically and the angles geometrically; or the angles arithmetically and the legs geometrically.

85. If, in the place of the straight lines, which form the legs, in any of the examples given, are substituted lines which in themselves induce movement, the feeling of Rhythm may be still further increased, provided the directions of movement are consistent.

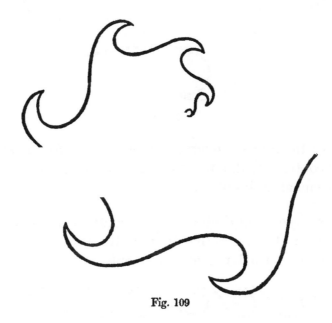

Fig. 109

In this case the movement is in the direction of increasing concentration and in the direction of the convergences.

If the movement of the convergences be contrary to the movement of concentration, there will be in the figure a contrary motion which may diminish or even entirely prevent the feeling of Rhythm. If the movement in one direction or the other predominates, we may still get the feeling of Rhythm, in spite of the drawback of the other and contrary movement.

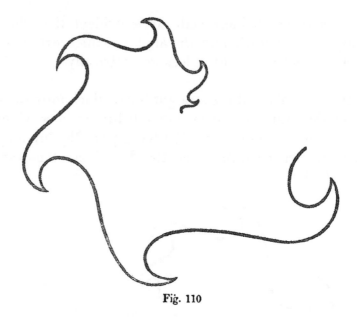

Fig. 110

In this case the linear convergences substituted for the straight lines are contrary to the direction of increasing concentration. The movement is doubtful.

86. Corresponding rhythms, set in contrary motion, give us the feeling of Balance rather than of Rhythm. The balance in such cases is a balance of movements.

Fig. 111

This is an example of corresponding and opposed rhythms producing the feeling, not of Rhythm, but of Balance.

ATTITUDES

LINES IN DIFFERENT ATTITUDES

87. Any line or linear progression may be turned upon a center, and so made to take an indefinite number and variety

of attitudes. It may be inverted upon an axis, and the inversion may be turned upon a center producing another series of attitudes which, except in the case of axial symmetry in the line, will be different from those of the first series.

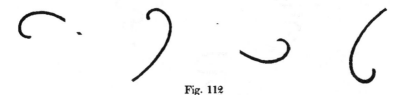

Fig. 112

In this case the line changes its attitude.

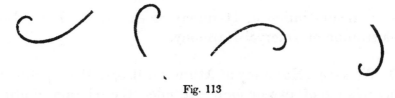

Fig. 113

In this case I have inverted the line, and turning the inversion upon a center I get a different set of attitudes.

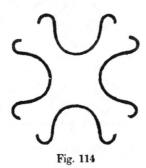

Fig. 114

In this case, which is a case of axial symmetry in the line, the inversion gives us no additional attitudes.

THE ORDER OF HARMONY IN THE ATTITUDES OF LINES

88. When any line or linear progression is repeated, without change of attitude, we have a Harmony of Attitudes.

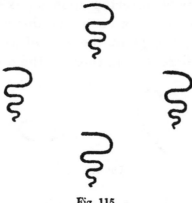

Fig. 115

This is an illustration of Harmony of Attitudes. It is also an illustration of Interval-Harmony.

89. We have a Harmony of Attitudes, also, in the repetition of any relation of two or more attitudes, the relation of attitudes being repeated without change of attitude.

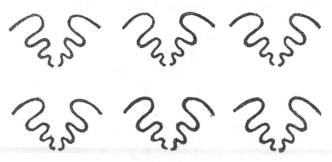

Fig. 116

We have here a Harmony of Attitudes due to the repetition of a certain relation of attitudes, without change of attitude.

THE ORDER OF BALANCE IN THE ATTITUDES OF LINES

90. When a line or linear progression is inverted upon any axis or center, and we see the original line and its inversion side by side, we have a Balance of Attitudes.

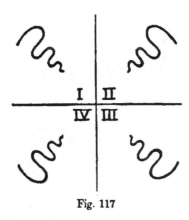

Fig. 117

The relation of attitudes I, II, of III, IV, and of I, II, III, IV, is that of Symmetrical Balance on a vertical axis. The relation of attitudes I, IV, and of II, III, is a relation of Balance but not of Symmetrical Balance. This is true, also, of the relation of I, III and of II, IV. Double inversions are never symmetrical, but they are illustrations of Balance. The balance of double inversions is central, not axial. These statements are all repetitions of statements previously made about positions.

THE ORDER OF RHYTHM IN THE ATTITUDES OF LINES

91. It often happens that a line repeated in different attitudes gives us the sense of movement. It does this when the grouping of the repetitions suggests instability. The movement is rhythmical when it exhibits a regularity of changes in the attitudes and in the intervals of the changes.

Fig. 118

In this case we have a movement to the right, but no Rhythm, the intervals being irregular.

Fig. 119

In this case the changes of attitude and the intervals of the changes being regular, the movement becomes rhythmical. The direction of the rhythm is clearly down-to-the-right.

92. In the repetition of any line we have a Harmony, due to the repetition. If the line is repeated in the same attitude, we have a Harmony of Attitudes. If it is repeated in the same intervals, we have a Harmony of Intervals. We have Harmony, also, in the repetition of any relation of attitudes or of intervals.

We have not yet considered the arrangement or composition of two or more lines of different measures and of different shapes.

THE COMPOSITION OF LINES

93. By the Composition of Lines I mean putting two or more lines together, in juxtaposition, in contact or interlacing. Our object in the composition of lines, so far as Pure Design is concerned, is to achieve Order, if possible Beauty, in the several modes of Harmony, Balance, and Rhythm.

HARMONY IN THE COMPOSITION OF LINES

94. We have Harmony in line-compositions when the lines which are put together correspond in all respects or in some respects, when they correspond in attitudes, and when there is a correspondence of distances or intervals.

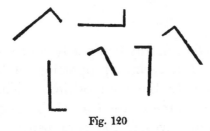

Fig. 120

In this case the lines of the composition correspond in tone, measure, and shape, but not in attitude; and there is no correspondence in distances or intervals.

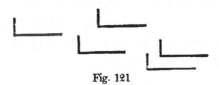

Fig. 121

In this case the attitudes correspond, as they did not in Fig. 120. There is still no correspondence of intervals.

Fig. 122

Here we have the correspondence of intervals which we did

not have either in Fig. 120 or in Fig. 121. There is not only
a Harmony of Attitudes and of Intervals, in this case, but
the Harmony of a repetition in one direction, Direction-Harmony. In all these cases we have the repetition of a certain
angle, a right angle, and of a certain measure-relation between the legs of the angle, giving Measure and Shape-Harmony.

95. The repetition in any composition of a certain relation
of measures, or of a certain proportion of measures, gives
Measure-Harmony to the composition. The repetition of
the relation one to three in the legs of the angle, in the illustrations just given, gives to the compositions the Harmony
of a Recurring Ratio. By a proportion I mean an equality
between ratios, when they are numerically different. The
relation of one to three is a ratio. The relation of one to
three and three to nine is a proportion. We may have in any
composition the Harmony of a Repeated Ratio, as in Figs.
120, 121, 122, or we may have a Harmony of Proportions, as
in the composition which follows.

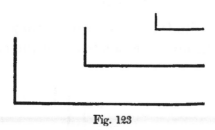

Fig. 123

96. To be in Harmony lines are not necessarily similar in
all respects. As I have just shown, lines may be in Shape-
Harmony, without being in any Measure-Harmony. Lines
are approximately in harmony when they correspond in
certain particulars, though they differ in others. The more
points of resemblance between them, the greater the harmony.
When they correspond in all respects we have, of course,
a perfect harmony..

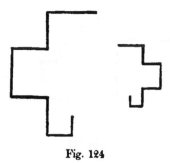

Fig. 124

This is a case of Shape-Harmony without Measure-Harmony and without Harmony of Attitudes.

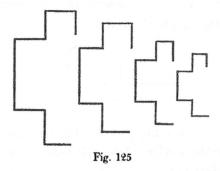

Fig. 125

In this case we have a Harmony of Shapes and of Attitudes, without Measure-Harmony or Harmony of Intervals. This is a good illustration of a Harmony of Proportions.

Straight lines are in Harmony of Straightness because they are all straight, however much they differ in tone or measure. They are in Harmony of Measure when they have the same measure of length. The measures of width, also, may agree or disagree. In every agreement we have Harmony.

Angular lines are in Harmony when they have one or more angles in common. The recurrence of a certain angle in different parts of a composition brings Harmony into the composition. Designers are very apt to use different angles when there is no good reason for doing so, when the repetition of one would be more orderly.

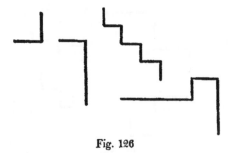

Fig. 126

The four lines in this composition have right angles in common. To that extent the lines are in Harmony. There is also a Harmony in the correspondence of tones and of width-measures in the lines. Considerable Harmony of Attitudes occurs in the form of parallelisms.

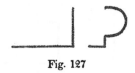

Fig. 127

These two lines have simply one angle in common, a right angle, and the angle has the same attitude in both cases. They differ in other respects.

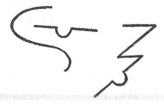

Fig. 128

In these three lines the only element making for Harmony, except the same tone and the same width, is found in the presence in each line of a certain small arc of a circle. Straightness occurs in two of the lines but not in the third. There is a Harmony, therefore, between two of the lines from which the third is excluded. There is, also, a Harmony of Attitude in these two lines, in certain parallelisms.

BALANCE IN THE COMPOSITION OF LINES

97. Lines balance when in opposite attitudes. We get Balance in all inversions, whether single or double.

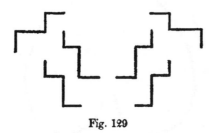

Fig. 129

Here similar lines are drawn in opposite attitudes and we get Measure and Shape-Balance. In the above case the axis of balance is vertical. The balance is, therefore, symmetrical. Symmetrical Balance is obtained by the single inversion of any line or lines on a vertical axis. Double inversion gives a Balance of Measures and Shapes on a center. We have no Symmetry in double inversions. All this has been explained.

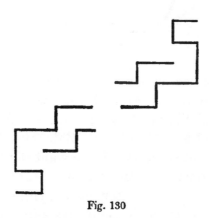

Fig. 130

We have Measure and Shape-Balance on a center in this case. It is a case of double inversion. It is interesting to turn these double inversions on their centers, and to observe the very different effects they produce in different attitudes.

98. Shapes in order to balance satisfactorily must be drawn in the same measure, as in Fig. 131 which follows.

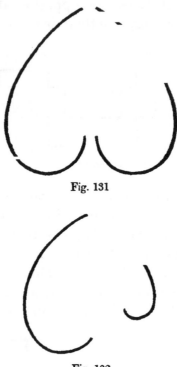

Fig. 131

Fig. 132

Here, in Fig. 132, we have Shape-Harmony without Measure-Harmony. It might be argued that we have in this case an illustration of Shape-Balance without Measure-Balance. Theoretically that is so, but Shape-Balance without Measure-Balance is never satisfactory. If we want the lines in Fig. 132 to balance we must find the balance-center between them, and then indicate that center by a symmetrical inclosure. We shall then have a Measure-Balance (occult) without Shape-Balance.

99. When measures correspond but shapes differ the balance-center may be suggested by a symmetrical inclosure or framing. When that is done the measures become balanced.

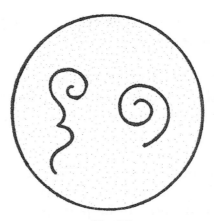

Fig. 133

Here we have Measure-Harmony and a Measure-Balance without Shape-Harmony or Shape-Balance. The two lines have different shapes but the same measures, lengths and widths corresponding. The balance-center is found for each line. See pp. 54, 55. Between the two centers is found the center, upon which the two lines will balance. This center is then suggested by a symmetrical inclosure. The balancing measures in such cases may, of course, be turned upon their centers, and the axis connecting their centers may be turned in any direction or attitude, with no loss of equilibrium, so far as the measures are concerned.

Fig. 134

The Balance of Measures here is just as good as it is in Fig. 133. The attitudes are changed but not the relation of

the three balance-centers. The change of shape in the inclosure makes no difference.

100. Measure-Balance without Shape-Harmony or Shape-
Balance is satisfactory only when the balance-center is un-
mistakably indicated or suggested, as in the examples which
I have given.

101. There is another form of Balance which is to be
inferred from what I have said, on page 18, of the Balance
of Directions, but it needs to be particularly considered and
more fully illustrated. I mean a Balance in which directions or inclinations to the right are counteracted by corresponding or equivalent directions or inclinations to the left.
The idea in its simplest and most obvious form is illustrated
in Fig. 22, on page 18.   In that case the lines of inclination correspond. They do not necessarily correspond except
in the extent of contrast, which may be distributed in various
ways.

Fig. 135

The balance of inclinations in this case is just as good as the
balance in Fig. 22. There is no symmetry as in Fig. 22.
Three lines balance against one. The three lines, however,
show the same extent of contrast as the one. So far as the
inclinations are concerned they will balance in any arrangement which lies well within the field of vision. The eye must
be able to appreciate the fact that a disposition to fall to the

right is counteracted by a corresponding or equivalent disposition to fall to the left.

Fig. 136

This arrangement of the inclining lines is just as good as the arrangement in Fig. 135. The inclinations may be distributed in any way, provided they counteract one another properly.

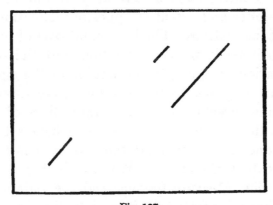

Fig. 137

In this case I have again changed the composition, and having suggested the balance-center of the lines, as attractions, by a symmetrical inclosure, I have added Measure-Balance (occult) to Inclination-Balance. The Order in Fig. 137 is greater than the Order in Figs. 135 and 136. In Fig. 137 two forms of Balance are illustrated, in the other cases only one. The value of any composition lies in the number of orderly connections which it shows.

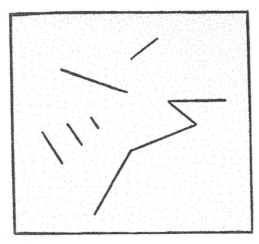

Fig. 138

In this case I have taken a long angular line and added a
sufficient number and extent of opposite inclinations to make
a balance of inclinations. The horizontal part of the long line
is stable, so it needs no counteraction, but the other parts
incline in various degrees, to the left or to the right. Each
inclining part requires, therefore, either a corresponding line
in a balancing direction, or two or more lines of equivalent
extension in that direction. In one case I have set three lines
to balance one, but they equal the one in length, that is to
say, in the extent of contrast. We have in Fig. 138 an illustration of occult Measure-Balance and the Balance of Ineli-
nations. I have illustrated the idea of Inclination-Balance by
very simple examples. I have not considered the inclinations
of curves, nor have I gone, at all, into the more difficult problem of balancing averages of inclination, when the average
of two or more different inclinations of different extents of
contrast has to be counteracted. In Tone-Relations the
inclinations are of tone-contrasts, and a short inclination with
a strong contrast may balance a long inclination with a slight
one, or several inclinations of slight contrasts may serve to
balance one of a strong contrast. The force of any inclining
line may be increased by increasing the tone-contrast with

the ground tone. In tone-relations the problem becomes complicated and difficult. The whole subject of Inclination-Balance is one of great interest and worthy of a separate treatise.

RHYTHM IN THE COMPOSITION OF LINES

102. We will first consider the Measure-Rhythms which result from a gradual increase of scale, an increase in the extent of the contrasts. The intervals must, in such Rhythms, be regular and marked. They may be equal; they may alternate, or they may be regularly progressive.

Fig. 139

In this case I feel that the direction of the Rhythm is up-to-the-right owing to the gradual increase of length and couse-quently of the extent of contrast in the lines, in that direction.

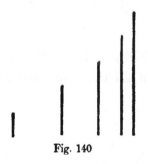

Fig. 140

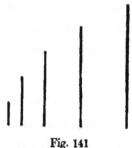

Fig. 141

In this case a greater extension of contrasts pulls one way and a greater crowding of contrasts the other. I think that crowding has the best of it. The movement, though much retarded, is, I feel, down-to-the-left rather than up-to-the-right, in spite of the fact that the greater facility of reading to the right is added to the force of extended contrasts.

103. Substituting unstable for stable attitudes in the examples just given, we are able to add the movement suggested by instability of attitude to the movement caused by a gradual extension of contrasts.

Fig. 142

The movement up-to-the-right in Fig. 139 is here connected with an inclination of all the lines down-to-the-right.

Fig. 143

Here the falling of the lines down-to-the-left counteracts the movement in the opposite direction which is caused by the extension of contrasting edges in that direction. A crowding together of the lines, due to the diminution of intervals toward the left, adds force to the movement in that direction.

Fig. 144

In this case a movement up is caused by convergences, a movement down by crowding. The convergences are all up, the crowding down. I think that the convergences have it. I think the movement is, on the whole, up. The intervals of the crowding down diminish arithmetically.

Fig. 145

The convergences and the crowding of attractions are, here, both up-to-the-right. The Rhythm is much stronger than it was in Fig. 144. The intervals are those of an arithmetical progression.

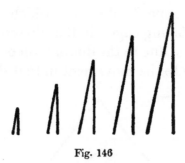

Fig. 146

The movement here is up-to-the-right, because of convergences in that direction and an extension of contrasts in that direction.

Fig. 147

In this case the two movements part company. One leads the eye up-to-the-left, the other leads it up-to-the-right. The movement as a whole is approximately up. As the direction of the intervals is horizontal, not vertical, this is a case of movement without Rhythm. The movement will become rhythmic only in a vertical repetition. That is to say, the direction or directions of the movement in any Rhythm and the direction or directions of its repetitions must coincide. In Fig. 139, the movement is up-to-the-right, and the intervals may be taken in the same direction, but in Fig. 147 the movement is up. The intervals cannot be taken in that direction. It is, therefore, impossible to get any feeling of Rhythm from the composition. We shall get the feeling of Rhythm only when we repeat the movement in the direction of the movement, which is up.

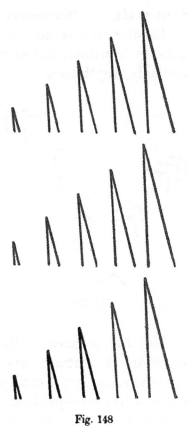

Fig. 148

vertical repetition of the composition given in
result is an upward movement in regular and
s, answering to our understanding of Rhythm.

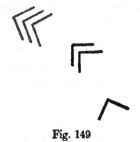

Fig. 149

spaced at regular intervals, the movement is in regular and marked measures. Its direction is due to an increase in the number of attractions, to crowding, and to convergences. The movement is, accordingly, rhythmical.

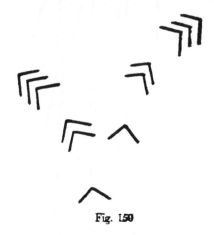

Fig. 150

The movement of Fig. 149 is here partly destroyed by an inversion and opposition of attitudes and directions. The movement is, on the whole. up. but it can hardly be described as rhythmical, because it has no repetition upwards, as it has in the next illustration. Fig. 151. Before proceeding, however, to the consideration of Fig. 151, I want to call the attention of the reader to the fact that we have in Fig. 150 a type of Balance to which I have not particularly referred. It is a case of unsymmetrical balance on a vertical axis. The balancing shapes and movements correspond. They incline in opposite directions. They diverge equally from the vertical axis. The inclinations balance. At the same time the composition does not answer to our understanding of Symmetry. It is not a case of right-and-left balance on the vertical axis. The shapes and movements are not right and left and opposite. One of the shapes is set higher than the other. The balance is on the vertical. It is obvious, but it is not symmetrical. It is a form of Balance which has many and very interesting possibilities.

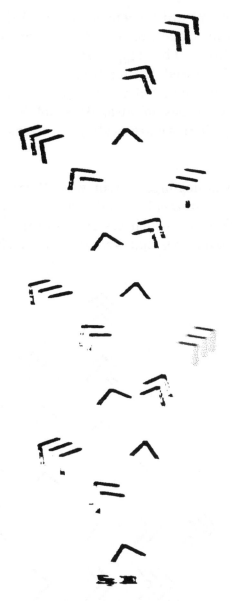

The repetition, as this case of somewhat contrary movements, a repetition at equal intervals on a vertical axis, gives us more balance than Harden. We feel, however, a general upward movement through the repetitions and, as this movement implies, it must be described as rhythmical.

The feeling of upward movement in Fig. 151 is, no doubt, partly due to the suggestion of upward growth in certain forms of vegetation. The suggestion is inevitable. So far as the movement is caused by this association of ideas it is a matter, not of sensation, but of perception. The consideration of such associations of ideas does not belong, properly, to Pure Design, where we are dealing with sense-impressions, exclusively.

104. Rhythm is not inconsistent with Balance. It is only necessary to get movements which have the same or nearly the same direction and which are rhythmical in character to balance on the same axis and we have a reconciliation of the two principles.

Fig. 152

Here we have a **Rhythm**, of somewhat **contrary** movements, with Balance, — Balance on a diagonal axis. The Balance is not satisfactory. The Balance of Inclinations is felt more than the Balance of Shapes.

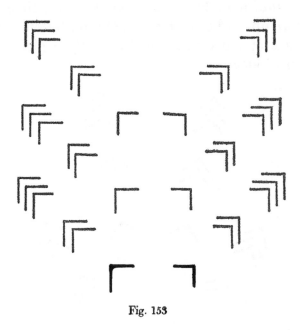

Fig. 153

In this case we have the combination of a Rhythm of somewhat contrary, but on the whole upward, movements with Symmetry.

If the diverging movements of Fig. 153 should be made still more diverging, so that they become approximately contrary and opposite, the feeling of a general upward movement will disappear. The three movements to the right will balance the three movements to the left, and we shall have an illustration of Symmetrical Balance, with no Rhythm in the composition as a whole. It is doubtful whether the balance of contrary and opposite movements is satisfactory. Our eyes are drawn in opposite directions, away from the axis of balance, instead of being drawn toward it. Our appreciation of the balance must, therefore, be diminished. Contrary and opposite movements neutralize one another, so we have neither rest nor movement in the balance of contrary motions.

By bringing the divergences of movement together, gradually, we shall be able to increase, considerably, the upward
movement shown in Fig. 153.   At the same time, the suggestion of an upward growth of vegetation becomes stronger.
The increase of movement will be partly explained by this
association of ideas.

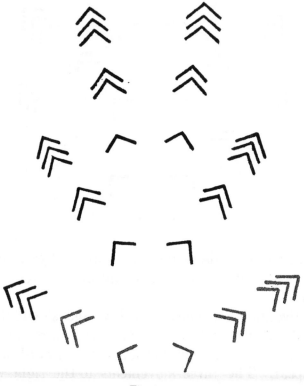

Fig. 154

Here all the movements are pulled together into one direction.
The Rhythm is easier and more rapid. The Balance is just
as good. The movement in this case is no doubt facilitated
by the suggestion of upward growth. It is impossible to
estimate the force which is added by such suggestions and
associations.

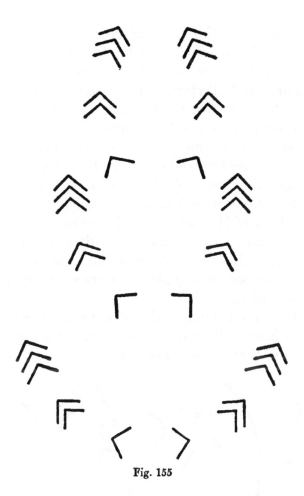

Fig. 155

Here the movements come together in another way.

The number and variety of these illustrations might, of course, be indefinitely increased. Those which I have given will, I think, serve to define the principal modes of line-composition, when the lines are such as we choose to draw.

THE COMPOSITION OF VARIOUS LINES

orderly composition, the problem becomes one of doing the best we can with our terms. We try for the greatest possible number of orderly connections, connections making for Harmony, Balance, and Rhythm. We arrange the lines, so far as possible, in the same directions, giving them similar attitudes, getting, in details, as much Harmony of Direction and of Attitudes as possible, and establishing as much Harmony of Intervals as possible between the lines. By spacing and placing we try to get differences of character as far as possible into regular alternations or gradations in which there will be a suggestion either of Harmony or of Rhythm. A suggestion of Symmetry is sometimes possible. Occult Balance is possible in all cases, as it depends, not upon the terms balanced, but upon the indication of a center of attractions by a symmetrical framing of them.

Let us take seven lines, with a variety of shape-character, with as little Shape-Harmony as possible, and let us try to put these lines together in an orderly way.

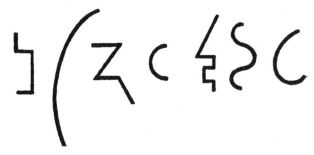

Fig. 156

With these lines, which show little or no harmony of character, which agree only in tone and in width-measure, lines which would not be selected certainly as suitable material for orderly compositions, I will make three compositions, getting as much Order into each one as I can, just to illustrate what I mean. I shall not be able to achieve a great deal of Order, but enough, probably, to satisfy the reader that the effort has been worth while.

Fig. 157

In this case I have achieved the suggestion of a Symmetrical
Balance on a vertical axis with some Harmony of Directions
and of Attitudes and some Interval-Harmony.

Fig. 158

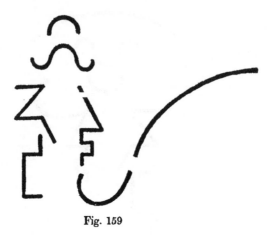

Fig. 159

Here is another arrangement of the same terms. Fortunately, in all of these cases, the lines agree in tone and in width-measure. That means considerable order to begin. with.

This problem of taking any terms and making the best possible arrangement of them is a most interesting problem, and the ability to solve it has a practical value. We have the problem to solve in every-day life; when we have to arrange, as well as we can, in the best possible order, all the useful and indispensable articles we have in our houses. To achieve a consistency and unity of effect with a great number and variety of objects is never easy. It is often very difficult. It is particularly difficult when we have no two objects alike, no correspondence, no likeness, to make Harmony. With the possibility of repetitions and inversions the problem becomes comparatively easy. With repetitions and inversions we have the possibility, not only of Harmony, but of Balance and Rhythm. With inversions we have the possibility, not only of Balance, but of Symmetrical Balance, and when we have that we are not at all likely to think whether the terms of which the symmetry is composed are in harmony or not. We feel the Order of Symmetry and we are satisfied.

Fig. 160

In this design I repeat an inversion of the arrangement in Fig. 158. The result is a symmetry, and no one is likely to ask whether the elements of which it is composed are harmonious or not.   By inversions, single and double, it is possible to achieve the Order of Balance, in all cases.

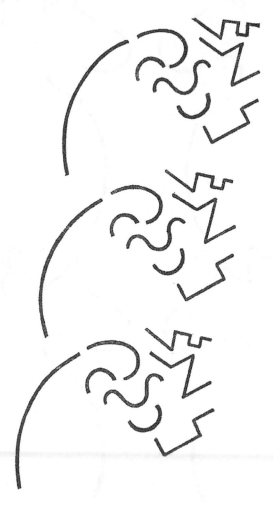

Fig. 161

For this design I have made another arrangement of my seven lines. The arrangement suggests movement. In repeating the arrangement at regular and equal intervals, without change of attitude, I produce the effect of Rhythm. Without resorting to inversion, it is difficult to make even an approximation to

Symmetry with such terms (see Fig. 157), but there is little or no difficulty in making a consistent or fairly consistent movement out of them, which, being repeated at regular intervals, without change of attitude, or with a gradual change of attitude, will produce the effect of Rhythm.

Up to this point I have spoken of the composition of lines in juxtaposition, that is to say, the lines have been placed near together so as to be seen together. I have not spoken of the possibilities of Contact and Interlacing. The lines in any composition may touch one another or cross one another. The result will be a composition of connected lines. In certain cases the lines will become the outlines of areas. I will defer the illustration of contacts and interlacings until I come to consider the composition of outlines.

OUTLINES

106. OUTLINES are lines which, returning to themselves, make inclosures and describe areas of different measures and shapes. What has been said of lines may be said, also, of outlines. It will be worth while, however, to give a separate consideration to outlines, as a particularly interesting and important class of lines.

As in the case of dots and lines, I shall disregard the fact that the outlines may be drawn in different tones, making different contrasts of value, color, or color-intensity with the ground-tone upon which they are drawn. I shall, also, disregard possible differences of width in the lines which make the outlines. I shall confine my attention, here, to the measures and shapes of the outlines and to the possibilities of Harmony, Balance, and Rhythm in those measures and shapes.

HARMONY, BALANCE, AND RHYTHM IN OUTLINES

107. What is Harmony or Balance or Rhythm in a line is Harmony, Balance, or Rhythm in an Outline.

Fig. 162

In this outline we have Measure-Harmony in the angles, Measure-Harmony of lengths in the legs of the angles, Measure and Shape-Balance on a center and Symmetry on the vertical axis. The same statement will be true of all polygons which are both equiangular and equilateral, when they are balanced on a vertical axis.

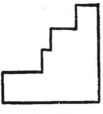

Fig. 163

In this case we have Measure-Harmony of angles but no Measure-Harmony of lengths in the legs of the angles. We have lost Measure and Shape-Balance on a center which we had in the previous example.

Fig. 164

In this case the angles are not all in a Harmony of Measure; but we have Measure-Harmony of lengths in the legs of the angles, and we have Measure and Shape-Balance on a center. There is a certain Harmony in the repetition of a relation of two angles.

Fig. 165

In this case we have Measure-Harmony in the angles, which are equal, and a Harmony due to the repetition of a certain measure-relation in the legs of the angles. As in Fig. 162, we háve here a Measure and Shape-Balance on a center and Symmetry on the vertical axis. This polygon is not equilateral, but its sides are symmetrically disposed. Many interesting and beautiful figures may be drawn in these terms.

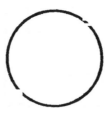

Fig. 166

We have in the circle the most harmonious of all outlines. The Harmony of the circle is due to the fact that all sections of it have the same radius and equal sections of it have, also, the same angle-measure. The circle is, of course, a perfect illustration of Measure and Shape-Balance on a center. The balance is also symmetrical. We have a Harmony of Directions in the repetition of the same change of direction at every point of the outline, and we have a Harmony of Distances in the fact that all points of the outline are equally distant from the balance-center, which is unmistakably felt.

Fig. 167

The Ellipse is another example of Measure and Shape-Balance on a center. In this attitude it is also an illustration of Symmetry.

Fig. 168

In this case we still have balance but no symmetry. The attitude suggests movement. We cannot help feeling that the figure is falling down to the left. A repetition at equal intervals would give us Rhythm.

Fig. 169

In this case we have an outline produced by the single inversion of a line in which there is the repetition of a certain motive in a gradation of measures. That gives Shape-Harmony without Measure-Harmony. This is a case of Symmetrical Balance. It is also a case of rhythmic movement upward. The movement is mainly due to convergences.

Fig. 170

In this case, also, the shapes repeated on the right side and on the left side of the outline show movements which become in repetitions almost rhythmical. The movement is up in spite of the fact that each part of the movement is, in its ending, down. We have in these examples symmetrical balance on a vertical axis combined with rhythm on the same axis. It may be desirable to find the balance-center of an outline when only the axis is indicated by the character of the outline.

it is. Regarding the outline as a line of attractions, the eye is presumably held at their balance-center, wherever it is. Exactly where it is is a matter of visual feeling. The balance-center being ascertained, it may be indicated by a symmetrical outline or inclosure, the center of which cannot be doubtful.

Fig. 171

The balance-center, as determined by visual feeling, is here clearly indicated. In this case besides the balance on a center we have also the Symmetry which we had in Fig. 169.

Fig. 172

The sense of Balance is, in this case, much diminished by the change of attitude in the balanced outline. We have our balance upon a center, all the same; but the balance on the vertical axis being lost, we have no longer any Symmetry. It will be observed that balance on a center is not inconsistent with movement. If this figure were repeated at equal intervals without change of attitude, or with a gradual change, we should have the Rhythm of a repeated movement.

In some outlines only certain parts of the outlines are orderly, while other parts are disorderly.

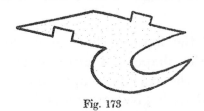

Fig. 173

In the above outline we have two sections corresponding in measure and shape-character and in attitude. We have, therefore, certain elements of the outline in harmony. We feel movement but not rhythm in the relation of the two curves. There is no balance of any kind.

We ought to be able to recognize elements of order as they occur in any outline, even when the outline, as a whole, is disorderly.

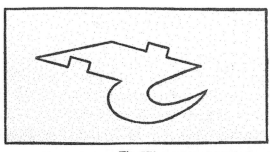

Fig. 174

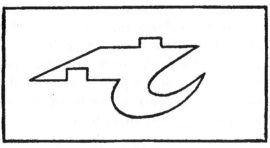

Fig. 175

The attitude of the figure is here made to conform, as far as possible, to the shape and attitude of the symmetrical framing: this for the sake of Shape and Attitude-Harmony. The change of attitude gives greater stability.

INTERIOR DIMENSIONS OF AN OUTLINE

108. A distinction must be drawn between the measures of the outline, as an outline, and the measures of the space or area lying within the outline: what may be called the interior dimensions of the outline.

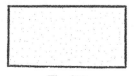

Fig. 176

In this case we must distinguish between the measures of the outline and the dimensions of the space inclosed within it. When we consider the measures — not of the outline, but of the space or area inside of the outline — we may look in these measures, also, for Harmony, for Balance, or for Rhythm, and for combinations of these principles.

HARMONY IN THE INTERIOR DIMENSIONS OF AN OUTLINE

109. We have Harmony in the interior dimensions of an outline when the dimensions correspond or when a certain relation of dimensions is repeated.

Fig. 177

In this case we have an outline which shows a Harmony in the correspondence of two dimensions.

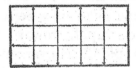

Fig. 178

In this case we have Harmony in the correspondence of all vertical dimensions, Harmony in the correspondence of all horizontal dimensions, but no relation of Harmony between the two. It might be argued, from the fact that the interval in one direction is twice that in the other, that the dimensions have something in common, namely, a common divisor. It is very doubtful, however, whether this fact is appreciable in the sense of vision. The recurrence of any relation of two dimensions would, no doubt, be appreciated. We should have, in that case, Shape-Harmony.

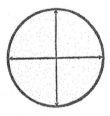

Fig. 179

In this circle we have a Measure-Harmony of diameters.

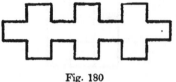

Fig. 180

In this case we have a Harmony due to the repetition of a certain ratio of vertical intervals: 1:3, 1:3, 1:3.

110. Any gradual diminution of the interval between opposite sides in an outline gives us a convergence in which the eye moves more or less rapidly toward an actual or possible contact. The more rapid the convergence the more rapid the movement.

Fig. 181

In this case we have not only symmetrical balance on a vertical axis but movement, in the upward and rapid convergence of the sides BA and CA toward the angle A. The question may be raised whether the movement, in this case, is up from the side BC to the angle A or down from the angle A toward the side BC. I think that the reader will agree that the movement is from the side BC into the angle A. In this direction the eye is more definitely guided. The opposite movement from A toward BC is a movement in diverging directions which the eye cannot follow to any distance. As the distance from BC toward A decreases, the convergence of the sides BA and CA is more and more helpful to the eye and produces the feeling of movement. The eye finds itself in a smaller and smaller space, with a more and more definite impulse toward A. It is a question whether the movement from BC toward A is rhythmical or not. The movement is not connected with any marked regularity of measures. I am inclined to think, however, that the gradual and even change of measures produces the feeling of equal changes in equal measures. If so, the movement is rhythmical.

When the movement of the eye in any convergence is a movement in regular and marked measures, as in the example which follows, the movement is rhythmical, without doubt.

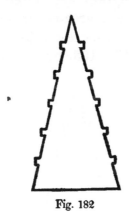

Fig. 182

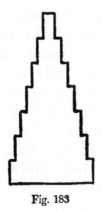

Fig. 183

In this case we have another illustration like Fig. 182, only the measures of the rhythm are differently marked. The force of the convergence is greatest in Fig. 181. It is somewhat diminished by the measure-marks in Fig. 182. It is still further diminished, in Fig. 183, by the angles that break the measures.

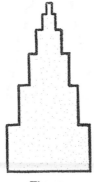

Fig. 184

In this case the movement is more rapid again, the measures being measures of an arithmetical progression. There is a crowding together of attractions in the direction of the convergence, and the movement is easier than it is in Fig. 183, in spite of the fact that the lines of convergence are more broken in Fig. 184. There is an arithmetical diminution of horizontal as well as of vertical lines in Fig. 184.

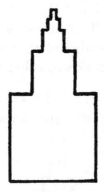

Fig. 185

In this case the measures of the rhythm are in the terms of a geometrical progression. The crowding together of attractions is still more rapid in this case and the distance to be traversed by the eye is shorter. The convergence, however, is less compelling, the lines of the convergence being so much broken — unnecessarily.

The movement will be very much retarded, if not prevented, by having the movement of the crowding and the movement of the convergence opposed.

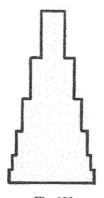

Fig. 186

the convergence upward and that of a crowding together of attractions downward. The convergence is stronger, I think, though it must be remembered that it is probably easier for the eye to move up than down, other things being equal.

111. The movements in all of these cases may be enhanced by substituting for the straight lines shapes which are in themselves shapes of movement.

Fig. 187

Here, for example, the movement of Fig. 184 is facilitated and increased by a change of shape in the lines, lines with move‑ ment being substituted for lines which have no movement, beyond the movement of the convergence.

Fig. 188

In Fig. 188 all the shapes have a downward movement which contradicts the upward movement of convergence. The movement down almost prevents the movement up.

112. The movement of any convergence may be straight, angular, or curved.

Fig. 189

In this case the movement of the convergence is angular. It should be observed that the movement is distributed in the measures of an arithmetical progression, so that we have, not only movement, but rhythm.

Fig. 190

In this case the movement of convergence is in a curve. The stages of the movement, not being marked, the movement is not rhythmical, unless we feel that equal changes are taking place in equal measures. I am inclined to think that we do feel that. The question, however, is one which I would rather ask than answer, definitely.

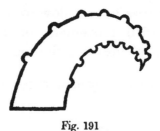

Fig. 191

In this case the movement is, unquestionably, rhythmical, because the measures are clearly marked. The measures are in an arithmetical progression. They diminish gradually in the direction of the convergence, causing a gradual crowding together of attractions in that direction.

Substituting, in the measures, shapes which have movement, the movement of the rhythm may be considerably increased, as is shown in the example which follows.

Fig. 192

This is a case in which the movement is, no doubt, facilitated by an association of ideas, the suggestion of a growth.

113. The more obvious the suggestion of growth, the more inevitable is the movement in the direction of it, whatever that direction is. It must be understood, however, that the movement in such cases is due to an association of ideas, not to the pull of attractions in the sense of vision. The pull of an association of ideas may or may not be in the direction of the pull of attractions.

Fig. 193

In Fig. 193 we have an illustration of a rhythmic movement upward. The upward movement is due quite as much
to an association of ideas, the thought of a growth of vegetation, as it is to mere visual attractions. It happens that the
figure is also an illustration of Symmetrical Balance. As we
have Harmony in the similarity of the opposite sides, the
figure is an illustration of combined Harmony, Balance, and
Rhythm.

There is another point which is illustrated in Fig. 193. It
is this: that we may have rhythmic movement in an outline,
or, indeed, in any composition of lines, which shows a gradual
and regular change from one shape to another; which shows
a gradual and regular evolution or development of shape-
character; provided the changes are distributed in regular
and marked measures and the direction of the changes, the
evolution, the development, is unmistakable; as it is in
Fig. 193. The changes of-shape in the above outline are

involves a comparison of shape with shape, so it is as much a matter of perception as of sensation. Evolutions and developments in Space, in the field of vision, are, as interesting as evolutions and developments in the duration of Time. When the changes in such movements are regular, when they take place in regular and marked measures, when we must take them in a certain order, the movements are rhythmical, whether in Time or in Space.

THE ATTITUDES OF OUTLINES

114. Any outline, no matter what dimensions or shape it has, may be turned upon a center and in that way made to take a great number and variety of attitudes. Not only may it be turned upon a center but inverted upon an axis. Being inverted, the inversion may be turned upon a center and made to take another series of attitudes, and this second series of attitudes will be different from the first series, except in cases of axial symmetry in the outline or area. It must be clearly understood that a change of attitude in any outline or area is not a change of shape.

115. What has been said of Harmony, Balance, and Rhythm in the attitudes of a line applies equally well to outlines and to the spaces defined by them.

THE ARRANGEMENT AND COMPOSITION OF OUTLINES

116. By the composition of outlines I mean putting two or more outlines in juxtaposition, in contact or interlacing. In all cases of interlacing, of course, the shape-character of the interlacing outlines is lost. The outlines become the outlines of other areas and of a larger number of them. Our object in putting outlines together is, in Pure Design, to illustrate the orders of Harmony, Balance, and Rhythm, to achieve Order, as much as we can, if possible Beauty.

I will now give a series of examples with a brief analysis or explanation of each one.

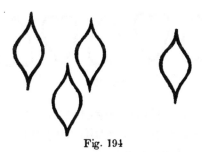

Fig. 194

In this case we have Shape-Harmony in the outlines and also a Harmony of Attitudes.

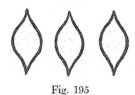

Fig. 195

Here we have another illustration of the Harmony of Shapes and of Attitudes, with a Harmony of Intervals, which we did not have in Fig. 194

Fig. 196

In this case we have a Harmony of Attitudes and of Intervals

Fig. 197

In this case we have a Harmony of Attitudes in the repetition of a relation of two opposite attitudes; this with Shape-Harmony and Interval-Harmony.

Fig. 198

In this case we have a Symmetry of Attitudes, with Shape-Harmony and Interval-Harmony. Turning the composition off the vertical axis we should have Balance but no Symmetry. The balance-center will be felt in all possible attitudes of this composition.

Fig. 199

In this case I have repeated a certain outline, which gives me the Harmony of a repetition, — this in connection with a progression in scale, so that the Harmony is Shape-Harmony, not Measure-Harmony. We have in the attitude of this repetition a Symmetrical Balance. The movement is rhythmical and the direction of the rhythm is up.

The movement in Fig. 199 might be indefinitely increased by the introduction into it of a gradation of attractions, increasing in number. That means that the extent of contrasting edges is increased from measure to measure.

Fig. 200

The addition of details, increasing in number from measure to measure upward, increases the movement of the rhythm in that direction.

Fig. 201

at diverging angles of sixty degrees, we get what may be called a radial balance upon the basis of a hexagon.

Outlines may be drawn one inside of the other or several inside of one.

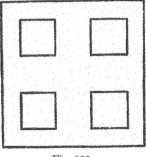

Fig. 202

This is a case of outlines-within-outlines and of Shape-Harmony without Measure-Harmony. There is, also, a Harmony of Attitudes, but no Harmony of Intervals.

Interesting results may be produced by drawing a series of outlines similar in shape, the second inside of the first, the third inside of the second, and so on.

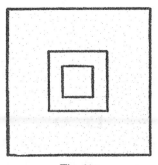

Fig. 203

In this case, for example, we have the outlines drawn one inside of the other. The outlines have all the same shape, but different measures. It is a case of Shape-Harmony and Harmony of Attitudes, without Measure-Harmony, and without any Harmony of Intervals. This is a very interesting and important form of Design which has many applications.

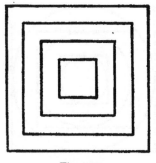

Fig. 204

In this case, also, we have Shape-Harmony without Measure-Harmony. We have a Harmony of Attitudes and also of Intervals, the spaces between the outlines corresponding.

Fig. 205

Here we have the Harmony of an alternation of Attitudes repeated, with Shape-Harmony, without Measure-Harmony.

In all forms of design in which we have the concentric repetition of a certain outline we have, in connection with the feeling of a central balance, the feeling of a movement or movements toward the center. These movements are due to convergences. Movements carrying the eye away from the center, in opposite directions, interfere with the feeling of balance. The feeling is enhanced, however, when the movements converge and come together.

We may have not only an alternation of attitudes in these

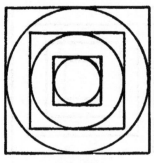

Fig. 206

The repetition of outlines-within-outlines may be coneen-
tric or eccentric. The repetition is concentric in Fig. 204.
It is eccentric in the example which follows.

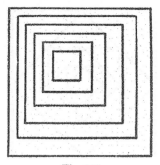

Fig. 207

In all eccentric repetitions like this we have a lack of balance
and the suggestion of movement. The direction of the movement is determined by the direction of convergences and of
the crowding together of attractions. The movement in Fig.
207 is up-to-the-left, unmistakably. Repeating the composition of Fig. 207, at regular intervals and without change of
attitude, the movement up-to-the-left would be extended to
the repetitions and the movement would be rhythmical. The
movement is rhythmical in the composition itself, as shown
in Fig. 207, because the movement in the composition is regular in character, regular in its measures, and unmistakable in
direction.

Fig. 208

This is another example of eccentric repetition in outlines-within-outlines. As in Fig. 207, we have movement, and the movement is rhythmical.

In the examples I have given there have been no contacts and no interlacings. Contacts and interlacings are possible.

Fig. 209

Here, for an example, is an instance of contact, with Harmony of Attitudes and a Symmetrical Balance on a vertical axis.

Fig. 210

In this case we have contacts, with no Harmony of Attitudes.

The balance which is central as well as axial is in this attitude of the figure symmetrical.

Fig. 211

Here we have a similar composition with interlacings.

When the outlines have different shapes as well as different
measures, particularly when the outlines are irregular and the
shapes to be put together are, in themselves, disorderly, the
problem of composition becomes more difficult. The best
plan is to arrange the outlines in a group, making as many
orderly connections as possible. Taking any composition of
outlines and repeating it in the different ways which I have
described, it is generally possible to achieve orderly if not
beautiful results.

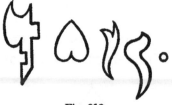

Fig. 212

Here are five outlines, very different in shape-character. Let
us see what can be done with them. A lot of experiments
have to be tried, to find out what connections, what arrangements, what effects are possible. The possibilities cannot
be predicted. Using tracing-paper, a great many experiments
can be tried in a short time, though it may take a long time
to reach the best possible results.

Fig. 213

In this example I have tried to make a good composition with
my five outlines. The problem is difficult. The outlines to
be combined have so little Harmony. The only Harmony we
can achieve will be the Harmony of the same arrangement of
shapes repeated, which amounts to Shape-Harmony. Inversions will give us the satisfaction of Balance. Inversions on
a vertical axis will give us the satisfaction of Symmetry. In
the design above given I have achieved simply the Harmony
of a relation of shapes repeated, with Rhythm. The Rhythm
is due to the repetition of a decidedly unbalanced group of
elements with a predominance of convergences in one direction. The movement is on the whole up, in spite of certain
downward convergences. The upward convergences predominate. There are more inclinations to the right than to the
left, but the composition which is repeated is unstable in its
attitude and suggests a falling away to the left. The result-

Fig. 214

In this case I have less difficulty than in Fig. 213, having left out one of my five outlines, the one most difficult to use with the others. There is a great gain of Harmony. There is a Harmony of Intervals and a Harmony in the repetition of the same grouping of outlines. In the outlines themselves we have a Harmony of curved character, and the curves fit one another very well, owing to a correspondence of measure and shape-character in certain parts. In such cases we are able to get considerable Harmony of Attitudes into the composition. There is a Harmony of Attitudes in the repeats, as well as in certain details. Comparing Fig. 214 with Fig. 213, I am sure the reader will agree that we have in Fig. 214 the larger measure of Harmony.

Fig. 215

In Fig. 215 I have used inversions and repetitions of the rather disorderly outline which gave me so much difficulty when I tried to combine it with the other outlines. Whatever merit the composition has is due solely to the art of composition, to the presence of Attitude-Harmony, Interval-Harmony, and to the inversions and repetitions; inversions giving Balance, repetitions giving Harmony.

While it is important to recognize the limitation of the terms in this problem, it is important to yield to any definite impulse which you may feel, though it carries you beyond your terms. The value of a rule is often found in breaking it for a good and sufficient reason; and there is no better reason than that which allows you, in Design, to follow any impulse you may have, provided that it is consistent with the principles of Order.

Fig. 216

In this case an effort has been made to modify the terms already used so as to produce a more rapid and consistent movement. Advantage has been taken of the fact that the eye is drawn into all convergences, so all pointing down has been, so far as possible, avoided. The movement is distinctly rhythmical.

In the previous examples I have avoided contacts and interlacing. It was not necessary to avoid them.

Fig. 217

117. What is done, in every case, depends upon the designer who does it. He follows the suggestions of his imagination, not, however, with perfect license. The imagination acts within definite limitations, limitations of terms and of principles, limitations of certain modes in which terms and principles are united. In spite of these limitations, however, if we give the same terms, the same principles, and the same modes to different people, they will produce very different results. Individuality expresses itself in spite of the limitation of terms and modes, and the work of one man will be very different from the work of another, inevitably. We may have Order, Harmony, Balance, or Rhythm in all cases, Beauty only in one case, perhaps in no case. It must be remembered how, in the practice of Pure Design, we aim at Order and hope

for Beauty. Beauty is found only in supreme instances of Order, intuitively felt, instinctively appreciated. The end of the practice of Pure Design is found in the love of the Beautiful, rather than in the production of beautiful things. Beautiful things are produced, not by the practice of Pure Design, but out of the love of the Beautiful which may be developed by the practice.

AREAS

118. I have already considered the measures of areas, in discussing the interior dimensions of outlines, and in discussing the outlines themselves I have considered the shapes of areas. It remains for me to discuss the tones in which the areas may be drawn and the tone-contrasts by which they may be distinguished and defined — in their positions, measures, and shapes.

LINEAR AREAS

119. Before proceeding, however, to the subject of tones and tone-relations, I must speak of a peculiar type of area which is produced by increasing or diminishing the width of a line. I have postponed the discussion of measures of width in lines until now.

A line may change its width in certain parts or passages. It may become wider or narrower as the case may be. The wider it is the more it is like an area. If it is sufficiently wide, the line ceases to be a line, and becomes an area. The line may change its width abruptly or gradually. The effect of the line is by these changes indefinitely varied. The line of Design is not the line of Geometry.

120. Considerable interest may be given to what I have called Linear Progressions by changing the width of the line at certain points, in certain passages, and more or less abruptly. The changes will be like accents in the line, giving variety and, possibly, an added interest.

Fig. 218

Let us take this line as the motive of a linear progression. We can give it a different character, perhaps a more interesting character, by widening all the vertical passages, as follows: —

Fig. 219

This is what we get for a motive by widening all the vertical passages.

Fig. 220

This is what we get for a motive by widening all the horizontal passages.

Fig. 221

Compare this Progression, in which I have used the motive of Fig. 219, with that of Fig. 77, p. 47. The accents, which in Fig. 221 occur in every repetition of the motive, might occur only in certain repetitions, at certain intervals.

Fig. 222

It is not necessary that the changes in the width of the line be abrupt, as in the examples just given. The width of the line may increase or diminish gradually, in which case we may have, not only accents in the line, but movements due to gradations of dimension, to convergences, or to an increase or gradual crowding together of attractions in a series of visual angles.

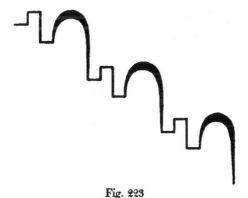

Fig. 223

In this case we have a gradual increase followed by a diminution of the width of the line in certain parts, and these changes occur at equal intervals. A certain amount of rhythmic movement is given to the progression by such accents, provided the direction of movement is unmistakable, which it is not in this case. It is not at all clear whether the

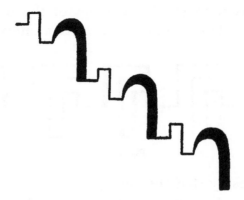

Fig. 224

In this case there is less doubt about the movement. It seems to be down-to-the-right. The eye is pulled through an increase of width-measures toward a greater extension and crowding together of contrasting edges.

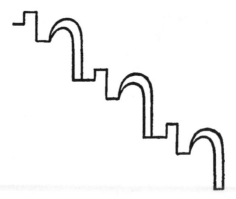

Fig. 225

Substituting outlines for areas in the previous illustration, we are surprised, perhaps, to find that the movement is reversed. We go up-to-the-left in this case, not down-to-the-right. The pull of a greater extension of tone-contrast in a given area was, in Fig. 224, sufficient to overcome the pull of a less evident convergence in the other direction.

By increasing or diminishing the width of lines, doing it

gradually or abruptly, we are able to control the movement of the eye to an indefinite extent. This is one of the important resources of the designer's art. Its use is not limited to forms of Linear Progression, but may be extended to all forms of Design in which lines are used.

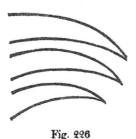

Fig. 226

In this case, for example, the eye follows the direction of convergences, but we can easily force it to turn and move in the opposite direction, by widening the lines in that direction, thus increasing the extent of contrasting edge until it more than outbalances the convergences; as in the following illustration: —

Fig. 227

THE ARRANGEMENT AND COMPOSITION OF AREAS

121. What has been said about the composition of Lines and Outlines applies equally well to the composition of Areas, so far as they are distinguished and defined by outlines. We will now proceed to consider areas as distinguished and defined, not by outlines, but by tone-contrasts. The composition of lines and outlines is one thing, the composition of

tones in different positions, measures,
In putting lines and outlines together
of view is that of drawing. In putting
tions, measures, and shapes we paint.
that of the painting.

TONES AND TONE-RELATIONS

122. UP to this point I have avoided the consideration of Tones and Tone-Relations. I have spoken of possible changes of tone in dots and in lines; changes of value, of color, of color-intensity; but it is not in dots nor in lines that these changes call for particular attention. Our interest has been in the positions, measures, shapes, and attitudes of dots and lines, and in the possibilities of arrangement and composition. When it comes to the consideration of areas and area-systems, however, the subject of tone-relations becomes one of the greatest interest, because areas are defined and distinguished, not only by their outlines, but quite as much by differences of tone; that is to say, by tone-contrasts.

THE PROCESS OF PAINTING AS DISTINGUISHED FROM DRAWING

123. The first thing to consider is the tone of the surface upon which you are going to paint. You then take a tone differing from the ground-tone, in value, in color, or in color-intensity, you put it in a certain position, and you spread it over a certain extent of space. In so doing you give to the space a certain shape. This is the process of Painting, as distinguished from the process of Drawing. In Drawing we think of lines and outlines first. In Painting we think of Tones first, of positions, measures, and shapes afterwards.

DEFINITION OF THE WORD TONE

124. In producing tones we use, necessarily, certain pigment-materials and mixtures of these materials. The effect of light produced by any particular material or mixture we call its tone. Though I have been using the word *Tone* I have not yet defined its meaning. I will now do that.

TONE-ANALYSIS, — VALUE, COLOR, INTENSITY, NEUTRALITY

125. In every tone we have to distinguish two elements, the quantity of light in it — what we call its value — and the quality of the light in it — its color; and the color, whatever it is, — Red, Orange, Yellow, Green, Blue, or Violet, — may be intense or neutral. By intensity I mean the quality of a color in its highest or in a very high degree. By the intensity of Red I mean Red when it is as red as possible. The mixture of Vermilion and Rose Madder, for example, gives us a Red of great intensity. That is about the strongest Red which we are able to produce with the pigment-materials which we use. Intensity must not be confounded with value nor value with intensity. By value I mean more or less light. By intensity I mean a great purity and brilliancy of color. Intensity stands in opposition to neutrality, in which no color can be distinguished. The more color we have in any tone the more intensity we have. The less the intensity the less color, and the absence of color means neutrality or grayness. Neutrality or grayness, though it is the negation of color, the zero of color, so to speak, must be classed as a color because upon analysis it proves to be a result of color combination or mixture. When I speak, as I shall from time to time, of the neutral as a color, it will be understood that I am speaking of a combination or mixture of colors in which no particular color can be distinguished. I speak of the neutral as a color just as I speak of zero as a number. We use zero as a number though it is no number, and counts for nothing.

STUDY OF TONES AND TONE-RELATIONS

126. The study of tones and tone-relations means the study of pigment-materials and their effects, to find out what quantities of light we can produce, what qualities of color, what intensities of color, what neutralizations. That is the problem of tones and tone-relations. We cannot know much about tones and tone-relations until we have had experience in the use of pigment-materials. We must be able to distinguish

tones, however slight the differences of value or of color or of color-intensity, and we must be able to produce tones according to our discriminations: this with exact precision. In order to think in tone-relations we must have definite ideas of tone and of tone-relations, in the form of visual images. In order to express our ideas we must be able to paint. We must have practice in painting and a great deal of it. I propose to describe this practice in tones and tone-relations: what it ought to be, what forms it should take.

PIGMENT-MATERIALS

127. Of pigments I use these: Blue Black, Madder Lake (Deep), Rose Madder, Indian Red, Venetian Red, Vermilion, Burnt Sienna, Cadmium Orange, Yellow Ochre, Pale Cadmium, Aureolin, Cremnitz White, "Emeraude" Green (Green Oxide of Chromium, transparent), Cobalt Blue, French Ultramarine Blue. These are the pigments which I suggest for oil-painting. In water-color painting I should substitute Charcoal Gray for Blue Black. "Emeraude Green" is often called Viridian in the form in which it is used in water-color. For Cremnitz White I should substitute, in water-color painting, Chinese White. These are the pigment-materials which I use myself and recommend to others. There are, of course, many other pigments which may be used, but these will, I think, be found sufficient for all purposes. Provided with these pigments, with a palette upon which to put them, with brushes and other materials necessary for painting, we are prepared to take up the study of tones and tone-relations.

THE SCALE OF VALUES

128. It is evident that we have in black paint the least quantity of light which we can produce. Black is the lowest of all values. It is equally evident that in white paint we have the greatest possible quantity of light. White is the highest of all values. Mixing Black and White in different proportions we can produce an indefinite number of intermediates. We do

not want, however, to be indefinite in our terms; on the contrary we want to be as definite as possible. Let us, therefore,
establish, between Black and White, a Middle Value (M);
between Black and Middle Value an intermediate Dark (D);
between Middle Value and White an intermediate Light (Lt),
and between these five values the intermediates, Low Dark
(LD), High Dark (HD), Low Light (LLt), and High Light
(HLt). Further intermediates (eight) may be established, but
to these we need not give any particular names. If we have
occasion to refer to any one of them we can say that it lies
between certain quantities or values of light for which we have
names. We can speak, for example, of the intermediate between Middle and High Dark, and it may be described in
writing by the formula M–HD. With this terminology we shall
be able to describe the principal quantities or values of light
both in speech and in writing.

In order to study the principal quantities or values of light
and the possibilities of contrast which they afford it is wise to
avoid all differences of color and color-intensity. To do that
we produce our Scale of Values in terms of perfect neutrality,
in which no color can be distinguished. When we use the
names of different values it is understood that they are values
of Neutrality. The term M, for example, stands for Neutral
Middle, D for Neutral Dark, Lt for Neutral Light.

CONTRASTS OF THE SCALE OF VALUES

129. Having produced a scale of nine neutral values, including White and Black, the question arises as to the number
of contrasts which it affords, and it is easy to see that the number is thirty-six.

The vertical lines in the following diagram indicate the possible contrasts of value in the Scale of Values. Counting the
lines, we see that the number of contrasts is thirty-six. Producing these contrasts, we shall see what each one amounts to.

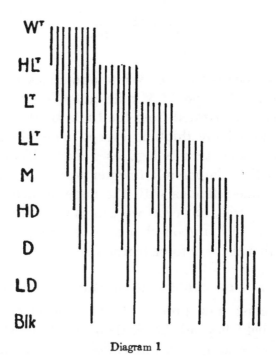

Diagram 1

DEFINITION OF VALUE-RELATIONS

130. The best method of describing and distinguishing these value-contrasts will be to use the value-names in a form of fractions. For example, $\frac{Lt}{D}$ would mean a contrast of Dark on Light, $\frac{D}{Lt}$ would mean a contrast of Light on Dark, $\frac{Wt}{Blk}$ would mean a contrast of Black on White. That is to say, White is subdivided or crossed by Black. When we wish to describe several contrasts in combination, we set the value of the ground-tone above the line, always, the value of the tone or tones put upon it below, thus: —

$$\frac{Lt}{Wt \qquad\qquad Blk}$$

$$\frac{\overline{\hspace{1cm}\text{Lt}\hspace{1cm}}}{\underset{\text{M}}{\text{Wt}}\hspace{2cm}\text{Blk}}$$

This formula means spots of White and Black on a ground-tone of Light, with a spot of Middle on the White, the Middle being altogether separated from the Light by the White.

There is no definite thinking except in definite terms, and without some such terminology as I have devised and described, it will be impossible to enter upon an experimental practice in value-relations with the hope of definite results. With definite terms, however, we can take up the practice in value-relations with a good chance of learning, in the course of time, all that there is to be learned.

SCALES OF COLORS IN DIFFERENT VALUES

131. We must now proceed to the consideration of the qualities of light beyond the Scale of Neutral Values, in the region of colors and color-intensities, — a region of tones which we have not yet explored.

It is evident that no color can exist either in the value of Black or in the value of White, but in every other value we have the possibility of all colors. That is to say, we may have Red (R) or Orange (O) or Yellow (Y) or Green (G) or Blue (B) or Violet (V) or any of the colors lying intermediate between them, — Red Orange (RO), Orange Yellow (OY), Yellow Green (YG), Green Blue (GB), Blue Violet (BV), or Violet Red (VR): all these, in any value of the Scale of Values, except in the value of Black and in the value of White. The possibilities of value and color, in tones, are exhibited in the following diagram: —

DIAGRAM OF VALUES AND COLORS

Wt													Wt
HLt	R	RO	O	OY	Y	YG	G	GB	B	BV	V	VR	HLt
Lt	R	RO	O	OY	Y	YG	G	GB	B	BV	V	VR	Lt
LLt	R	RO	O	OY	Y	YG	G	GB	B	BV	V	VR	LLt
M	R	RO	O	OY	Y	YG	G	GB	B	BV	V	VR	M
HD	R	RO	O	OY	Y	YG	G	GB	B	BV	V	VR	HD
D	R	RO	O	OY	Y	YG	G	GB	B	BV	V	VR	D
LD	R	RO	O	OY	Y	YG	G	GB	B	BV	V	VR	LD
Blk													Blk

Diagram 2

DEFINITION OF THE COLOR-TERMS

132. It is important that the words which we use for the different colors should be well understood, that in using them we use them with the same meanings. By Red I mean the only positive color which shows no element either of Yellow or of Blue. It is the color which we often describe by the word crimson, and we produce it by the mixture of Rose Madder and Vermilion. By Yellow I mean the only positive color which shows no element either of Red or Blue. It is the color of the primrose which may be produced by the pigment Aureolin. By Blue I mean the only positive color which shows no element either of Yellow or of Red. Blue is seen in a clear sky after rain and in the pigment Cobalt. By Orange I mean a positive color showing equal elements of Red and of Yellow. By Green I mean a positive color showing equal elements of Yellow and of Blue. By Violet I mean a positive color showing equal elements of Blue and Red. The character of the intermediates is clearly indicated by their several names. In each one we see the adjacents in equal measures. This definition of the

colors is only approximate. It does not pretend to be scientific, but it may help to bring us to a common understanding. To carry these definitions farther, I should have to produce examples. This I can do in my class-room, producing each color according to my idea, exactly. I might reach the same result approximately by color-printing, but the result would not, probably, be permanent. The samples produced by hand, for use in the class-room, can be reproduced from time to time when they no longer answer to the ideas which they are intended to express. In this treatise I shall use a terminology instead of colored illustrations which would not be satisfactory, or, if satisfactory, not so permanently.

COLOR-INTENSITIES IN DIFFERENT VALUES

133. If we proceed to carry out the idea of Diagram 2, producing all the twelve colors in all of the seven values intermediate between the extremes of Black and White, making the colors, in every case, as strong, as intense, as is possible with the pigment-materials we have chosen to use, we shall discover that the twelve colors reach their greatest intensities in different values; that is to say, in different quantities of light. Red reaches its greatest intensity in the value High Dark, Orange in Low Light, Yellow in High Light, Green in Low Light, Blue in High Dark, Violet in Low Dark, approximately; and the intermediate colors reach their greatest intensities in the intermediate values, approximately. In order to indicate this fact in our diagram, we will mark the positions of greatest intensity by putting the color signs in larger type.

DIAGRAM OF VALUES, COLORS, AND COLOR–INTENSITIES

Wt														Wt
HLt	R	RO	O	OY	Y	YG	G	GB	B	BV	V	VR	HL
Lt	R	RO	O	OY	Y	YG	G	GB	B	BV	V	VR	Lt
LLt	R	RO	O	OY	Y	YG	G	Gb	B	BV	V	VR	LLt
M	R	RO	O	OY	Y	YG	G	GB	B	BV	V	VR	M
HD	R	RO	O	OY	Y	YG	G	GB	B	BV	V	VR	HD
D	R	RO	O	OY	Y	YG	G	GB	B	BV	V	VR	D
LD	R	RO	O	OY	Y	YG	G	GB	B	BV	V	VR	LD
Blk													Blk

Diagram 3

TONES OF THE SPECTRUM AND OF PIGMENTS

134. It is probable that we have in the Spectrum an indication of the natural value-relations of the different colors when in their highest intensities. Owing to the limitations of pigment-material, however, it is impossible to reproduce the intensities of the Spectrum satisfactorily. An approximation is all that we can achieve in painting.

THE SPECTRUM SEQUENCE AND THE CIRCUIT OF THE COLORS

clearly enough, and Violet-Red is a connecting link between Violet and Red.

THE COMPLEMENTARIES

136. Considering the circuit of the colors which we are able to produce with our pigment-materials, the question arises, What contrasts of color are the strongest? what interval in the Scale of Colors gives us the strongest possible color-contrast? Producing the twelve colors in the values of their greatest intensities, and as intense as possible, and setting the tones in a circuit and in their natural and inevitable order, you will observe that the greatest color-contrast is the contrast between colors at the interval of the seventh: for example, the contrasts of Red and Green, or Orange and Blue, or Yellow and Violet. The colors at the interval of the sixth are less strong in contrast. The contrast diminishes gradually as we pass from the interval of the seventh to the interval of the second. The contrast of colors at the interval of the seventh, the greatest possible contrast, is called the contrast of the complementaries. In estimating intervals we count the colors between which the intervals occur.

A GENERAL CLASSIFICATION OF TONES

137. Taking each color in the value of its greatest intensity (as shown in the Spectrum), and as intense as possible, the color may be neutralized in the direction of Black (neutral darkness) or White (neutral light) or in the direction of any value of neutrality intermediate between Black and White, including the value of the color in its greatest intensity. If we think of five degrees of neutralization, including the extremes of Intensity and Neutrality, we shall get as definite a terminology for color-intensities and color-neutralizations as we have for colors and for values. The choice of five degrees is arbitrary. It is a question how far the classification shall go, what it shall include. We are dealing with infinity, and our limitations are necessarily arbitrary.

In Diagram 4 we have a general classification of tones as to value, color, color-intensity, and color-neutralization. Of values we have nine. Of colors we have twelve. Of degrees of intensity and of neutralization we have five.

COLOR-INTENSITIES AND COLOR-NEUTRALIZATIONS

138. It is important to distinguish between degrees of intensity and degrees of neutralization. The degrees of color-intensity and of color-neutralization, in any value, are described by fractions. The formula D–R$\frac{3}{4}$ means, value Dark, color Red, intensity three quarters. The formula D-R, $\frac{3}{4}$N means, value Dark, color Red, three quarters neutralized. The formula M–O$\frac{1}{2}$ means, value Middle, color Orange, intensity one half. The formula M–O, $\frac{1}{2}$N means, value Middle, color Orange, half neutralized. M–O, $\frac{1}{2}$N is a tone somewhat less intense in color than M–O$\frac{1}{2}$, as may be seen on the diagram. The degree of neutralization has reference, in all cases, to the maximum intensity for the given value. What that is, theoretically, may be seen by referring to the triangle of the color, in which the possibilities of intensity, in different values, are clearly indicated.

THE DEFINITION OF PARTICULAR TONES

139. To define any tone, in this classification, we must name its value, its color, and the degree of color-intensity or neutralization.

THE CLASSIFICATION OF TONES NECESSARILY THEORETICAL

140. The general classification of tones in which is shown all the possibilities of value, color, color-intensity, and color-neutralization, in reflecting pigments, is necessarily theoretical, or rather ideal, because the degrees of intensity obtainable in any value depend upon the pigment-materials we have

Blue and White to produce it. It is only when we use the
most brilliant pigments — the Madders, Vermilion, the Cad-
miums, Aureolin, and Cobalt Blue — that we can approximate toward the highest intensities, as indicated in our
diagram and exhibited in the Spectrum.

THE DEFINITION OF PARTICULAR TONE-RELATIONS

141. The number of tone-contrasts — contrasts of value,
of color, and of color-intensity or neutralization—is, evi-
dently, beyond calculation.

The method of describing any particular contrast or contrasts is easy to understand. We have only to define the tones
and to indicate how they cross one another.

$$\frac{\text{RO, }\frac{1}{2}\text{N}}{\text{VR}}$$

This formula means that a spot of Violet-Red (Dark, full
intensity) is put on a ground-tone of Middle Red-Orange,
half neutralized.

$$\frac{\text{RO}\frac{1}{2}}{\dfrac{\text{VR}}{\text{YG}} \quad \text{Wt}}$$

This formula means that spots of Low Dark Violet-Red (full
intensity) and White are put on a ground-tone of Middle
Red-Orange, half intensity, and that on the spot of Low
Dark Violet-Red (full intensity), as a ground-tone, is put a
spot of Light Yellow-Green (full intensity). It is not necessary to name the value when the color occurs in the value
of its greatest intensity, and it is not necessary to describe
the intensity, in any value, when the greatest intensity possible to that value is meant. In the first case the value is
understood, in the second case the intensity — the greatest
for the value — is understood.

SEQUENCES OF VALUES AND COLORS

142. WHEN, in view of all possible tones, as indicated in the general classification of tones, according to value, color, and color-intensity, or color-neutralization (Diagram of the Triangles), we try to think what tones we shall use, what contrasts of tone we shall produce, we are sure to be very much "at sea," because of the great number and variety of possibilities. Even when we disregard differences of intensity and consider simply the possibilities of value and of color, as shown in the general classification of tones according to value and color (Diagram of Values and Colors, p. 137), we have still too many possibilities to consider, and our choice of tones is determined by accident or habit rather than by clear vision or deliberate preference. We shall find it worth while to limit our range in each experiment to some partieular sequence of values and colors, or to some particular combination of sequences. Instead of trying to think in the range of all values, all colors, we ought to limit our thinking, in each case, to the range of a few values and a few colors, — a few definite tones with which we can become perfectly familiar and of which we can have definite visual images. It is only when we can imagine tones vividly that we can think satisfactorily in tone-relations. We shall achieve this power of thinking in tones and tone-relations best through self-imposed limitations.

143. We ought to begin our study of Tones and Tone-Relations with the Scale of Neutral Values (see p. 135). We ought to work with the nine tones of this scale or sequence until we know them well, until we can visualize them clearly, and until we can produce them accurately; until we can readily produce any single tone of the scale and any of the thirty-six possible contrasts which the scale affords.

Besides the Scale of Neutral Values there are three types of
Value and Color Sequence which we may use.

144. First. We have the sequences which may be described
as those of the Vertical; sequences which may be indicated by
vertical lines drawn across the Diagram of Values and Colors.
In each of these sequences, twelve in number, we have one
color in all the values of the Scale of Values, except Black and
White. These sequences of the Vertical, as I shall call them,
are of very little use in Pure Design. They give us value-contrasts and contrasts of color-intensity (intensities of one color),
but no color-contrasts, no differences of color. The tones in
these sequences are monotonous in color.

145. Second. We have the sequences which may be described as those of the Horizontal; sequences which may be
indicated by horizontal lines drawn across the Diagram of
Values and Colors. In these sequences we have differences
of color and color-intensity, but all in one value. These
sequences give us color-contrasts (different colors in different
degrees of intensity), but no value-contrasts. The tones in
these sequences are monotonous in value. The sequences of
one horizontal are of very little use.

146. Third. We have the sequences which may be described as those of the Diagonal; sequences which may be
indicated by lines drawn diagonally across the Diagram of
Values and Colors. In drawing these sequences the reader
must not forget that the Scale of Colors is a circuit, so when
he reaches the end of the diagram he returns and continues
from the other end. The diagram might, for convenience in
drawing these sequences, be extended to several repetitions
of the Scale of Colors. In the sequences of the Diagonal we
have contrasts both of value and of color. The color in these
sequences changes from value to value through the Scale of
Values. Each sequence gives us certain colors in certain

values, and in no case have we two colors in the same value. To these sequences of the Diagonal we must give our particular attention. They are the sequences which we shall use constantly, in Representation as well as in the practice of Pure Design.

147. The sequences of the Diagonal fall into two divisions. First, there are the sequences which we draw through the Diagram of Values and Colors from Black up-to-the-right to White. I shall call these the Sequences of the Right Mode (Sign ▱). Second, there are the sequences which we draw from Black up-to-the-left to White. I shall call these the Sequences of the Left Mode (Sign ◱).

Taking the lowest color in the sequence as the keynote, we have for the Right Mode, in the Scale of Twelve Colors, twelve distinct sequences of which this which follows is. an example.

Seq. LD–BV, ▱ 2ds

	Wt	
HLt	–	OY
Lt	–	O
LLt	–	RO
M	–	R
HD	–	VR
D	–	V
LD	–	BV
	Blk	

In this sequence the colors are taken at the interval of the second. That is what is meant by the abbreviation 2ds.

Taking the lowest color of the sequence as its keynote, as before, we have for the Left Mode twelve distinct sequences, of which that which follows is an example.

Seq. LD–OY, ◻ 2ds

Wt

HLt	–	BV
Lt	–	V
LLt	–	VR
M	–	R
HD	–	RO
D	–	O
LD	–	OY

Blk

In this sequence, as in the one previously given, the colors are taken at the interval of the second.

148. The colors in these diagonal sequences may be taken not only at intervals of the second, but at intervals of the third, the fourth, the fifth, the sixth, and the seventh. Taking the colors at these different intervals we have, for each interval, twenty-four distinct sequences; twelve for the Right Mode, twelve for the Left Mode; in all one hundred and forty-four different sequences.

149. Among the sequences of the Diagonal those in which the colors are taken at the interval of the fifth are particularly interesting. The colors taken at the interval of the fifth fall into four triads,—the first, R–Y–B, the second, RO–YG–BV, the third, O–G–V, the fourth, OY–GB–VR. Taking the colors in any of these triads in the two modes, the Right and the Left, we get six sequences of different colors in different values for each triad. Of these Triad-Sequences I will give one as an example.

Seq. LD–R, ◻ 5ths

Wt

HLt	–	R
Lt	–	Y
LLt	–	B
M	–	R
HD	–	Y

The Triad-Scales, whether in the Right Mode or in the Left Mode, are of great interest both in Pure Design and in Representation. In Representation, however, the number of tones between the limits of Black and White would, as a rule, be increased, as in the extended diagram given farther on.

150. Instead of taking the colors at a certain interval in one mode or the other, it is possible to take the colors in a certain relation of intervals repeated; this in either mode. The relation of a third to a fifth, for instance, being repeated, in one mode or the other, gives us some very interesting sequences. The one which follows is an example.

LD–V, ▱ 5th–3d

Wt
HLt – ·Y
3d
Lt – O
5th
LLt – V
3d
M – B
5th
HD – Y
3d
D – O
5th
LD – V
Blk

The relation of a seventh followed by two fifths, when repeated, in either mode, gives a large number of sequences of very great interest, particularly for Representation.

151. Any two of the sequences which I have described as 'those of the Vertical, or more than two, may be combined and used together. In that case we have two or more colors to a value. The monotony which is inevitable in any single vertical sequence is avoided in the combination of two or more such sequences.

Seq. R and Seq. Y

	Wt	
R	HLt	Y
R	Lt	Y
R	LLt	Y
R	M	Y
R	HD	Y
R	D	Y
R	LD	Y
	Blk	

This is an example of the combination of two vertical sequences — the sequence of Red and the sequence of Yellow. I have not found the sequences of this type very interesting. In using them in Representation I have found it desirable to have the intensities increase gradually toward white, or, what amounts to the same thing, to have each color neutralized as it loses light. That happens, constantly, in Nature.

152. Any two of the sequences which I have described as of the Horizontal, or even more than two, may be combined and used together.

Seq. Lt and D, 3ds

| Lt | R | O | Y | G | B | V |
| D | R | O | Y | G | B | V |

This scale gives us a variety of color-contrasts with one value-contrast. The colors are taken at the interval of the third. They might be taken at any interval up to that of the seventh, in which case we should have a contrast of complementary colors in two values, each color occurring in each value. The monotony of value which is inevitable in any single horizontal sequence is in the combination of two or more such sequences avoided. I have used the Red-Yellow-Blue triad in three and in five values with satisfaction. Each value represents a plane of light in which certain differences of color are observed.

153. Any two of the sequences which I have described as of the Diagonal may be combined, in two ways. First, two sequences of the same mode may be combined. Second, two sequences of different modes, one of the Right Mode and one of the Left Mode, may be combined.

LD–GB ◥ 3ds with LD–RO ◥ 3ds

	Wt	
GB	HLt	RO
BV	Lt	OY
VR	LLt	YG
RO	M	GB
OY	HD	BV
YG	D	VR
GB	LD	RO
	Blk	

In this case we have a combination of two diagonal sequences of the Left Mode in which the colors are taken at the interval of the third. Changing the mode of these two sequences we get them inverted, thus: —

LD–GB ◪ LD–RO ◪ 3ds

	Wt	
GB	HLt	RO
YG	Lt	VR
OY	LLt	BV
RO	M	GB
VR	HD	YG
BV	D	OY
GB	LD	RO
	Blk	

Here the mode is changed and the combined sequences inverted. The combined sequences may be both in the same mode or in different modes. When the modes are different the sequences come into contact, and in some cases cross one another.

LD–V ▱ 2ds with LD–V ◺ 2ds

```
        Wt
         Y
    OY      YG
    O        G
    RO      GB
    R        B
    VR      BV
         V
        Blk
```

In this case we have a combination of two diagonal sequences. One of the sequences is in the Right, the other is in the Left Mode. The colors are in the values of their greatest intensities.

Seq. LD–GB ▱ 3ds with LD–GB ◺ 3ds

```
        Wt
        GB
    YG      BV
    OY      VR
        RO
    VR      OY
    BV      YG
        GB
        Blk
```

In this case the combined sequences cross one another in the tone of M–RO. The combined sequences have three tones in common. It may happen that the sequences combined will have no tones in common. This is shown in the sequence which follows: —

LD–O ◺ 5ths with LD–B ▱ 5ths

```
        Wt
    O   HLt   B
    G   Lt    Y
    V   LLt   R
    O   M     B
    G   HD    Y
    V   D     R
    O   LD    B
        Blk
```

154. Instead of having two colors to a value in the combination of two vertical sequences, we may have an alternation of colors in the values, giving one color to a value, thus: —

```
        Wt
  R    HLt
        Lt    Y
  R    LLt
        M     Y
  R    HD
        D     Y
  R    LD
        Blk
```

It has seemed to me that the sequences in which we have one color to a value give better results than those in which we have two or more colors to a value.

155. Instead of having each color in two values in the combination of two horizontal sequences, we may have the colors, taken at equal intervals, occurring alternately first in one value and then in the other.

```
Lt   R   .   Y   .   B   .
D    .   O   .   G   .   V
```

156. These alternating sequences may proceed, not only vertically and horizontally, but diagonally across the diagram. In that case the alternations will be between different value-intervals in a series of equal color-intervals or between different color-intervals in a series of equal value-intervals.

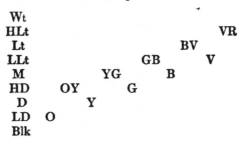

whole, **up**-to-the-right, is in the Right Mode. I have not used
any of the sequences, of this type, in which the value-intervals
alternate, first in one mode then in the other, with a constant
color-interval, but I have used, frequently, the alternation of
two different color-intervals in a series of equal value-intervals.
The sequences produced in this way are among the most interesting of all the many I have used. I will give several examples.

	Wt	
HLt	Y	
		7th
Lt	V	
		5th
LLt	O	
		7th
M	B	
		5th
HD	R	
		7th
D	G	
		5th
LD	V	
	Blk	

In this case the alternation is from the keynote, **Low Dark
Violet,** up first in the Left Mode a fifth, then up in the Right
Mode a seventh, then in the Left Mode a fifth, and so on up to
White. This particular alternation might be described as the
relation of a fifth and a seventh repeated, in the Left Mode.

	Wt	
HLt	Y	
		7th
Lt	V	
		5th
LLt	G	
		7th
M	R	
		5th
HD	B	
		7th
D	O	
		5th
LD	V	
	Blk	

In the sequence just given the alternation is, from the key-note Low Dark Violet, first in the Right Mode a fifth, then in the Left Mode a seventh: this through the Scale of Values up to White. The order of the previous sequence is inverted. This particular alternation might be described as the relation of a fifth and seventh repeated in the Right Mode.

The alternation of intervals of the fifth with intervals of the third gives some interesting sequences, in which the alternation of intervals is, necessarily, an alternation of modes.

	Wt	
HLt	Y	
		3d
Lt	G	
		5th
LLt	O	
		3d
M	Y	
		5th
HD	R	
		3d
D	O	
		5th
LD	V	
	Blk	

157. I have by no means exhausted the possibilities of value and color combination, but I have indicated a sufficient number to serve the purposes of experimental practice in tone-relations, for a long time to come. The sequences which I have found most interesting, in my own experiments, have been the diagonal sequences of the two modes, using intervals of the fifth, and the diagonal sequences in which with equal value-intervals there is an alternation of certain color-intervals, — the seventh and the fifth, and the seventh and two fifths. It may very well be that these particular sequences interest me because I have used them more than others and consequently think in them more easily.

but when it comes to the combination of Design with Representation, and particularly to Representation in Full Relief, it will be necessary to introduce intermediates into the Scale of Values. With this purpose in view I give one more diagram in which intermediates of value have been introduced. For convenience in drawing out the different sequences upon this diagram I have repeated the Scale of Colors showing the connection of Violet-Red with Red. This diagram (5) is simply an extension of the Diagram of Values and Colors given on p. 137.

159. We may use the various sequences I have described without mixing the tones, using the tones one at a time as they may be required; but if we choose we may mix adjacents or thirds or even threes. In that way the tone-possibilities of each sequence may be very much extended. It may be well to show what the extension amounts to by giving one of the sequences with an indication of the result of mixtures within the limits described.

Seq. LD–R ◺5ths

Wt	
HLt	R
Lt	Y
LLt	B
M	R
HD	Y
D	B
LD	R
Blk	

This is the sequence in which we decide to mix adjacents thirds, and threes.

A DIAGR

Wt									
	R	RO	O	OY	Y	YG	G	GB	B
HLt	R	RO	O	OY	Y	YG	G	GB	B
	R	RO	O	OY	Y	YG	G	GB	B
Lt	R	RO	O	OY	Y	YG	G	GB	B
	R	RO	O	OY	Y	YG	G	GB	B
LLt	R	RO	O	OY	Y	YG	G	GB	B
	R	RO	O	OY	Y	YG	G	GB	B
M	R	RO	O	OY	Y	YG	G	GB	B
	R	RO	O	OY	Y	YG	G	GB	B
HD	R	RO	O	OY	Y	YG	G	GB	B
	R	RO	O	OY	Y	YG	G	GB	B
D	R	RO	O	OY	Y	YG	G	GB	B
	R	RO	O	OY	Y	YG	G	GB	B
LD	R	RO	O	OY	Y	YG	G	GB	B
	R	RO	O	OY	Y	YG	G	GB	B
Blk									

ND COLORS

Wt

O	OY	Y	YG	G	GB	B	BV	V	VR	
O	OY	Y	YG	G	GB	B	BV	V	VR	HLt
O	OY	Y	YG	G	GB	B	BV	V	VR	
O	OY	Y	YG	G	GB	B	BV	V	VR	Lt
O	OY	Y	YG	G	GB	B	BV	V	VR	
O	OY	Y	YG	G	GB	B	BV	V	VR	LLt
O	OY	Y	YG	G	GB	B	BV	V	VR	
O	OY	Y	YG	G	GB	B	BV	V	VR	M
O	OY	Y	YG	G	GB	B	BV	V	VR	
O	OY	Y	YG	G	GB	B	BV	V	VR	HD
O	OY	Y	YG	G	GB	B	BV	V	VR	
O	OY	Y	YG	G	GB	B	BV	V	VR	D
O	OY	Y	YG	G	GB	B	BV	V	VR	
O	OY	Y	YG	G	GB	B	BV	V	VR	LD
O	OY	Y	YG	G	GB	B	BV	V	VR	

Blk

		2ds	3ds	3s
Wt				
HLt	R			
		O		
Lt	Y		V	N
		G		
LLt	B		O	N
		V		
M	R		G	N
		O		
HD	Y		V	N
		G		
D	B		O	N
		V		
LD	R			
Blk				

This diagram shows the results of mixing seconds, thirds, and threes. It is evident that in mixing the tones of any sequence in this way we go beyond the strict limitations of the sequence, particularly in mixing thirds and threes. The results obtained are fairly definite, however, and the tones obtainable are still within the range of definite thinking. If we should go farther, to the mixture of tones beyond the interval of the third, we should get into the region of indefinite possibilities.

160. It must be clearly understood that our object in using these sequences and more or less restricted mixtures is to limit our thinking so that it may gain in definiteness what it loses in extent. When we limit our thinking in any case to a few tones, — certain colors in certain values, — we come to know those tones so well that we can imagine any one of them vividly, without seeing it. It is only when we have in mind definite tone-images that we begin to think in tone-relations and rise to the possibilities of imaginative composition in tones.

gives the painter certain colors in certain values. That is to say, he has a certain number of tones to consider and to use. He takes one of the tones into his brush and gives it a position, a measure, and a shape. That done, he takes another tone and gives to that a position, measure, and shape. Proceeding in this way he creates a certain relationship of tones, positions, measures, and shapes, the terms of which relationship are perfectly definite. He repeats what he finds satisfactory. He avoids what he finds unsatisfactory. Experimenting in this way, in such definite terms, he ought to make a sure and steady progress toward the discovery of what is orderly and beautiful. The use of any particular sequence of values and colors is like the use, by the musician, of a well-tuned instrument. It is at once a definition of terms and a source of suggestion and of inspiration.

There is nothing occult or sacred about these sequences and combinations of sequences. In using them we are in no way safeguarded against error. Using these sequences, we can produce bad effects of light and of color as well as good ones. Whether the results of using these sequences are good or bad depends upon the user — what his thinking amounts to. It will be a grave mistake to regard any of these sequences as recipes for righteousness, when they are simply modes of thought. They are nothing more than the sections or divisions of a general classification of tones. In using any particular sequence we observe that the same value and color-relations recur repeatedly. That is always desirable from the point of view of Design. It means Harmony.

161. The beauty of any scheme of values and colors depends, not only upon the pigment-materials used, upon the sequence of values and colors chosen and upon the particular tones produced, but quite as much upon the relative positions and juxtapositions given to the tones, the quantities or measures in which they are used, and, lastly, the way in which the paint is handled. To find out what tones to use

as ground-tones, what tones to put upon these ground-tones, and in what quantities or measures, is a matter of experimental practice and of visual and imaginative discrimination.

Having defined the word tone and its elements, value, color, and color-intensity, and having established a general classification of tones to show the possibilities of tone, I must go on to describe what will be orderly in tone-relations. Order and Beauty in tone-relations will be found in Tone-Harmonies, Tone-Balances, and Tone-Rhythms.

162. By Tone-Harmony I mean a relation of likeness in tones. Tones are in Harmony when they resemble one another in all or in certain respects. To be in Harmony two or more tones must have at least something in common, either value or color. If they have the same color they may be in the same degree of intensity, giving a Harmony of Intensities. Tone-Harmony resolves itself into Value-Harmony, Color-Harmony, and the Harmony of Intensities. The Harmony of Intensities lies between tones of the same color, when they are equally neutralized or neutralized in approximately the same degree. When different colors are neutralized we have the Harmony of a common neutrality or grayness of color.

163. Tones may be harmonized on the palette before they are used, that is to say, before any positions, measures, and shapes are given to them on paper or canvas, or they may be harmonized after positions, measures, and shapes have been given to them. To harmonize tones on the palette, as to value, we must bring them approximately to the same value, with as little change of color as possible. To harmonize tones on the palette as to color we must bring them approximately to the same color, with as little change of value as possible. If two or more tones have the same color they may be intensified or neutralized until they are brought approximately to the same degree of intensity. The tones of Red showing a Harmony of Intensities would lie on a vertical line drawn through the triangle of Red in the Diagram of the Triangles.

As the tone-effect which we produce depends very largely upon the positions, measures, and shapes which we give to our tones, we may not be satisfied with an effect which has been produced with previously prepared and harmonized tones. We may wish to change the effect, to achieve a still greater Harmony. Given a certain arrangement or composition of tones, certain tones in certain positions, measures, and shapes, and given the problem to harmonize those tones, what do we do?

164. Suppose it is Value-Harmony which we want; what is our procedure?

```
        Wt
HLt  -  B
Lt   -  V
LLt  -  Y
M    -  RO
HD   -  G
D    -  O
LD   -  VR
       Blk
```

Here, let us say, are the tones of a design, certain colors in certain values. What shall we do with these tones to bring them into Value-Harmony?

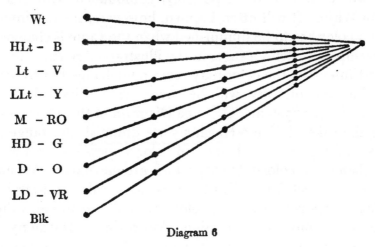

Diagram 6

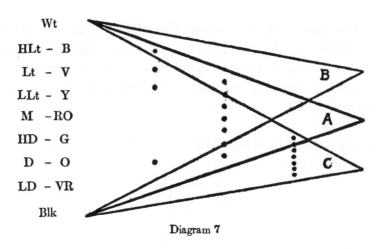

Diagram 7

Following the indications of this diagram, we pull the colors together toward Light in one case (B), toward Middle in another (A), toward Dark in a third (C). As we do this we increase the Value-Harmony. In reproducing the tones in a diminished range of values, raising the colors in value or lowering them, we are not obliged to change the colors except in cases where they become, possibly, confounded with Black or with White. It will often happen, however, that the intensity of a color has to be diminished when the value is changed. For example, if Red Orange, in the illustration given, is in its greatest intensity, the color may remain unchanged in System "A," but its intensity will be, necessarily, diminished in System "B," or System "C." See Diagram of the Triangles.

For the sake of Value-Harmony we diminish the range of values, making as little changes of color as possible, and only those changes of color-intensity which are inevitable. A complete and perfect Value-Harmony is, as a rule, undesirable because it means that all the colors are reduced to one value which gives a monotony of value. Approximate Harmony of Values is generally sufficient. The range of values is narrowed, the contrasts are diminished, and an even tonality is secured. That is all we require, in most cases, an approximation to one value.

165. Suppose it is Color-Harmony which we want to achieve: what procedure shall we follow?

Wt
B
V
Y
R
G
O
Blk

Here are certain tones, certain colors in certain values. What shall we do with these tones to get Color-Harmony? We must diminish the range of color-contrasts by giving predominance to one color, either to one of the colors to be harmonized or to some other. That may be done by mixing one color into all our tones.

Wt		Wt
B		V
V		VR
Y	Giving predominance to Red, we get:	O
R		R
G		N
O		RO
Blk		Blk

Diagram 8

The range of color-contrast is in this way diminished to the intervals between Violet, Orange, and Neutral. The process, so far as color is concerned, disregarding value-relations, is fully explained in the following diagram:—

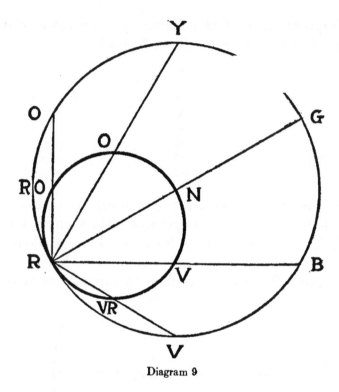

Diagram 9

Suppose, instead of giving predominance to Red, as in the example above, we give predominance to Blue, taking the same range of colors.

Wt		Wt
B		B
V		BV
Y	Giving predominance to Blue we get:	G
R		V
G		GB
O		N
Blk		Blk

Diagram 10

The range of color-contrast is in this way diminished to the intervals between Green, Violet, and Neutral. The process, so far as color is concerned, is fully explained in the following diagram: —

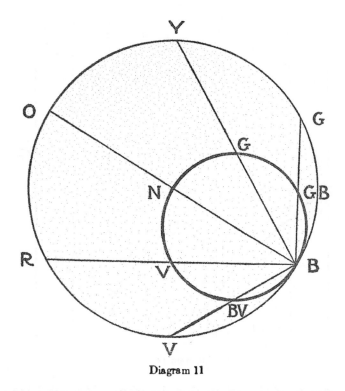

Diagram 11

In the diagrams which I have given the predominance is in the measure of one half. That is to say, the mixtures are half and half, theoretically speaking. The theoretical result is a range of intermediate colors. The predominance is not necessarily in the measure of one half. It may be in any measure. The presence of Red or Blue in all the tones may be hardly noticeable or it may amount to a general redness or blueness in which other colors are distinguished with more or less difficulty.

166. Suppose it is the harmony of grayness, a Harmony of Neutralization, which we want. What is the procedure to follow?

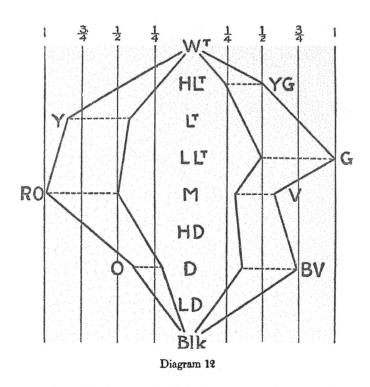

Diagram 12

The procedure is shown in this diagram. We see here what is meant by a Harmony of Neutralization, without changes of value. The neutralization is in the measure of one half in each case. Red Orange and Green are the only colors which exist in their maximum intensities. Their intensities are diminished to the half-point, without change of value, — from RO to RO$\frac{1}{2}$ in one case, and from G to G$\frac{1}{2}$ in the other. The other colors are reduced in their intensities proportionally. The value in each case remains unchanged.

167. Having considered the methods of getting Value-Harmony and Color-Harmony separately, I must now describe the method of getting the combination of Value-Harmony with the Harmony of Neutralization. To do this we must set the colors in positions regarding the Scale of Neutral Values, which will indicate their several values, and in each case the degree of intensity. We must then decide

whether to neutralize the several tones toward Black or
White, or toward some neutral value between these extremes.

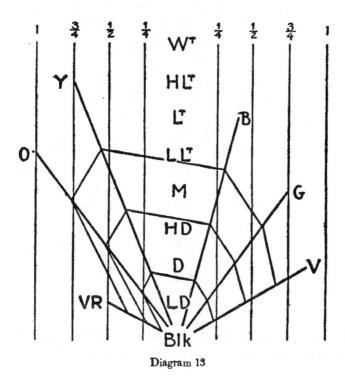

Diagram 13

This illustrates the method of a neutralization toward Black
in the measures of one quarter, one half, and three quarters.

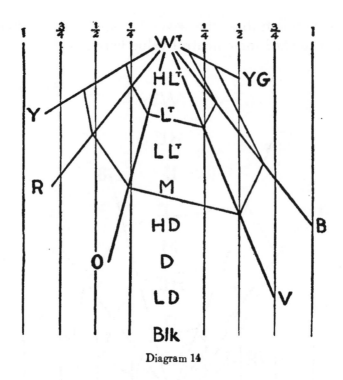

Diagram 14

This illustrates the method of a neutralization toward Whit in the measures of one third and two thirds.

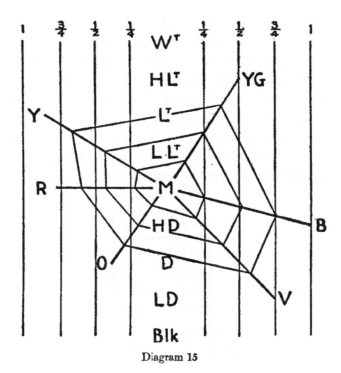

Diagram 15

This illustrates the method of a neutralization toward the Middle Neutral, between Black and White, a neutralization in the measures of one quarter, one half, and three quarters.

In bringing tones into harmony, by one or another or all of these various methods, we must remember that when we have diminished the contrast of value and of color beyond a certain point the result is monotony, a monotony which may be undesirable. It is easy to get into a state of mind in which we dislike all contrasts. In this state of mind we find no æsthetic satisfaction except in monotony. Such a state of mind should be avoided. Monotony is the Nirvana of æstheticism.

For example: I may repeat the contrast Orange-Blue any number of times in a certain composition. There is no Harmony of Value or of Color in the contrast, but in repeating the contrast I have the Harmony of a Repetition, just as I have a Harmony in the repetition of a certain line or outline in which there is no order of any kind. The Harmony lies solely in the repetition or recurrence. In this way I may repeat, at equal intervals all over a certain space, the various contrasts indicated by the following diagram: —

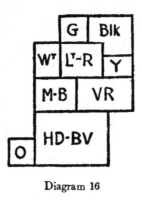

Diagram 16

There is no Harmony in the relation of tones here indicated, but we shall get Harmony in the repetition of this relation.

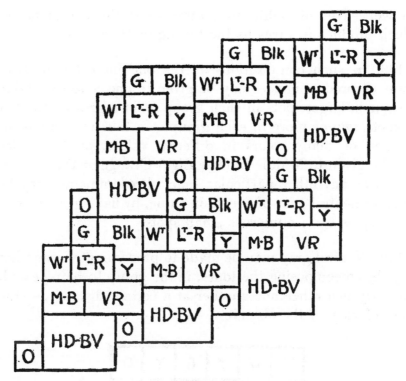

Diagram 17

all-over effect of light, no matter what the contrasts are which produce it, gives us the feeling of Harmony.

169. In such compositions as the one indicated in Diagram 17 predominance may be given to one tone by having it recur in larger spots in each group or in a greater number of spots, two or more in each group. In this way, in a composition of many colors in different values, predominance may be given to Middle Blue or Light Orange or Dark Blue-Violet, or any other particular tone. Predominance may be given to neutral gray of a certain value, by having it recur in larger spots or in numerous small spots.

170. Neutral gray may be made to predominate in another way; by so composing the tones, in the group to be repeated, that they neutralize one another at a certain distance, — the point of view of the observer.

Y	G	Y	G	Y	G
R	V	R	V	R	V
Y	G	Y	G	Y	G
R	V	R	V	R	V

Diagram 18

In this case Yellow and Violet will neutralize one another and Red will neutralize Green. The effect of the repetition of these complementary oppositions ought to be, at a certain distance, a very lively neutral.

It has been the idea of certain painters of our time to subject every tone-impression to analysis, and to produce the effect of the tone by an arrangement or composition of its elements. Many interesting and some beautiful results have been produced in this way.

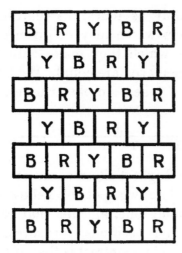

Diagram 19

In this case we have a repetition of the triad Red-Yellow-Blue, which, at a certain distance, ought to produce the effect of a middle neutral. The principle of these arrangements is one of the most important in tone-composition.

171. There is another consideration which ought to keep us from any morbid interest in harmonious monotonies, which ought to reconcile us to contrasts, even strong contrasts, and to a great variety in tones. Harmony is only one principle of composition in Design; we have two others which are equally important, — the principle of Balance and the principle of Rhythm. The principles of Balance and Rhythm are consistent with the greatest possible contrasts of tone. The tone-contrasts in forms of Balance and Rhythm may be strong, even harsh, and the appreciation and enjoyment of the Balance or of the Rhythm in no degree diminished.

We will now proceed to the consideration of Tone-Balance and Tone-Rhythm.

TONE-BALANCE

172. TONES, simply as tones, disregarding the positions, measures, and shapes which may be given to them, balance, when the contrasts which they make with the ground-tone upon which they are placed are equal. We have an indication of such a balance of tones, simply as tones, in the following formula: —

$$\frac{LD - V}{HLt - Y \qquad HLt - Y}$$

Two spots of High Light Yellow occur on a ground-tone of Low Dark Violet. The two spots of Yellow make equal contrasts with the ground-tone, and for that reason balance as tones, no matter what positions, measures, and shapes are given to them. The value-contrast is that of the interval of the seventh in the Scale of Values; the color-contrast is that of the interval of the seventh in the Scale of Colors. We must assume that the intensities are so adjusted as not to disturb the balance.

$$\frac{M - V}{Lt - O \qquad D - O}$$

In this case the values making the contrasts differ. The contrasts are, nevertheless, equal because the value-intervals are equivalent intervals. The value difference between Light and Middle is equivalent to the value difference between Dark and Middle. Though the contrasting elements differ, the contrasts are equal. In this case the contrasting colors are the same and the color-contrasts correspond. We must assume that the intensities are so adjusted as not to disturb the balance.

$$\frac{\text{LD} - \text{V}}{\text{LLt} - \text{O} \qquad \text{LLt} - \text{G}}$$

In this case the contrasting colors differ, but the contrasts are equal because the color-interval between Orange and Violet is the same as the color-interval between Green and Violet. In this case the value-contrasts correspond. We must assume here, as before, that there is no difference of color-intensity to disturb the balance.

$$\frac{\text{D} - \text{R}}{\text{HD} - \text{O} \qquad \text{LD} - \text{V}}$$

In this case the two tones which balance on the ground-tone differ both in value and in color. They balance, nevertheless, because both the value and the color-contrasts are of the interval of the third. Again we must assume that there is no disparity of intensities to disturb the balance.

173. The reader will find the Diagram of Values and Colors (No. 5) very useful in making calculations for tone-balances, so far as value-contrasts and color-contrasts are concerned, leaving out considerations of color-intensity.

Taking any tone indicated on the Diagram as a ground-tone, any tones at equal distances in balancing directions will balance on that ground-tone.

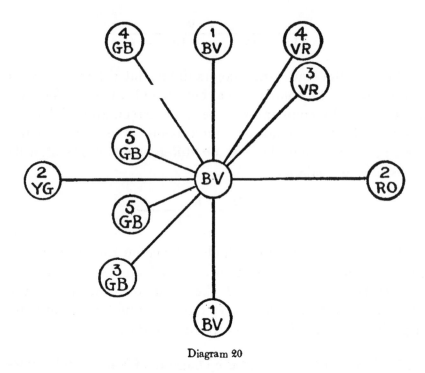

Diagram 20

The various types of tone-balance are shown in the above diagram. The tones which balance, one against the other, on the ground-tone of Blue-Violet, are the tones marked by the same number.

The value and color-balances being achieved, the intensities may be adjusted, increased or diminished, until the balance is perfect.

174. As you increase the color-intensity in any tone it attracts more attention, and unless you increase the intensity in the opposite tones there will be a disparity which will disturb your balance. When the intensity in any tone is too great, you can increase the color-contrast or the value-contrast of the opposite tones until the balance is achieved.

175. Up to this point I have been speaking of Tone-Balance in the abstract, of Tone-Balance as such. I have spoken of

Tone-Balance as something apart from Position, Measure, and Shape-Balance, as if tones could balance without having any positions, measures, or shapes assigned to them. The fact is that a tone does not exist until you give it a position, a measure, and a shape. It follows that Tone-Balance is, in all cases, more or less complicated by considerations of position, measure, and shape.

176. The principle of balance being that equal attractions balance at equal distances and unequal attractions at distances inversely proportional to them, it follows, that if the attraction of a tone is increased by quantity, the attraction of quantity may be balanced against the attraction of contrast. The calculation of such balances may be made on the Diagram of Values and Colors.

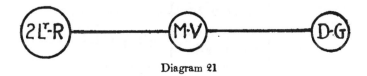

Diagram 21

In this case, for example, we have the indication of a possible balance of two parts of Light Red and one part of Dark Green on a ground-tone of Middle Violet, the difference of contrast in one case making up for a difference of quantity and of contrasting edge in the other.

177. So far as Tone-Balance depends upon positions, measures, and shapes, the problem is the problem of Position, Measure, and Shape-Balance, which we have already considered.

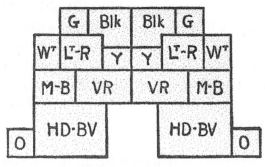

Diagram 22

In this case we have an instance of single inversion, which gives us a Symmetrical Balance, of tones, as well as of measures and shapes.

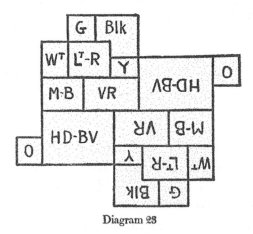

Diagram 23

In this case we have an instance of double inversion of tones, as well as of measures and shapes.

178. The tones and tone-contrasts on one side of a center or axis are not necessarily the same as those on the other side. We may have a Tone-Balance in which very different tones and tone-contrasts are opposed to one another. This brings us to the consideration of Occult Balance in Tones, Measures, and Shapes.

A balance of any tones and of any tone-contrasts, in any

measures and in any shapes, is obtained when the center of tone-attractions is unmistakably indicated, either by the symmetrical character of the balance or by a symmetrical inclosure which will indicate the center. Given any combination of tones, measures, and shapes, and the problem to find the balance-center, how shall we solve the problem? It cannot very well be done by reasoning. It must be done by visual feeling. The principle of Balance being clearly understood, finding the center of any tone-contrasts is a matter of experimental practice in which those persons succeed best who are most sensitive to differences of tone, and who make the greatest effort to feel the centers and to indicate them accurately. Experience and practice are necessary in all cases.

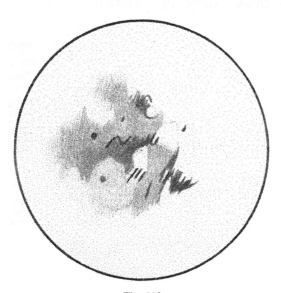

Fig. 228

ence of opinion. There is a center somewhere upon which the attractions are balancing. The question is, where is it? The illustration which I have given is in the terms of the Scale of Neutral Values. Differences of color and color-intensity would complicate the problem, but would not in any way affect the principle involved. I know of no more interesting problem or exercise than this: to achieve Tone-Balance where there is no Tone-Symmetry.

179. It will sometimes happen, that a gradation of tones or measures will draw the eye in a certain direction, toward the greater contrast, while a larger mass or measure of tone, on the other side, will be holding it back. In such a case we may have a mass balancing a motion.

Fig. 229

In this case the eye is drawn along, by a gradation of values, to the right, toward the edge of greater contrast, away from a large dark mass of tone in which there is no movement. The tendency of the dark mass is to hold the eye at its center. The problem is to find the balance-center between the motion and the mass. I have done this, and the balance-center is indicated by the symmetrical outline of the diagram.

such cases the attractions of tone or measure or shape on the
other side have to be increased if we are to have a balance.
Symmetrical shapes have a tendency to hold the eye at
centers and on axes. Given certain attractions on the other
side, we must be sure that they are sufficient to balance the
force of the symmetry in addition to the force of its tone-
contrasts, whatever they are.

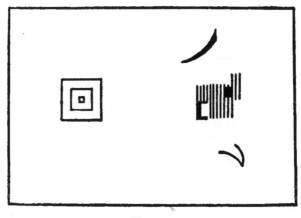

Fig. 230

In this case we have an approximate balance in which the
force of a symmetry, with contrasting edges, on one side, is
balanced by contrasts and certain movements on the other.
If I should turn down the upper spot on the right, we would
feel a loss of balance due to the turning of two movements,
which combine to make one movement to the right, into
two movements down to the right. If I should increase the
force of the symmetry, by filling in the center with black, it
would be necessary either to move the symmetry nearer to the
center or to move the opposite attractions away from it. An
unstable attitude in the symmetry would have to be counteracted, in some way, on the other side.

Intricate shapes from which the eye cannot easily or
quickly escape often hold the eye with a force which must
be added to that of their tone-contrasts.

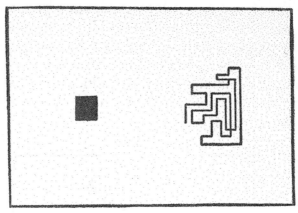

Fig. 231

In this case the shape on the right requires a pretty strong dark spot to balance its contrasts and its intricacy.

The problem is further complicated when there are, also, inclinations, to the right or to the left, to be balanced.

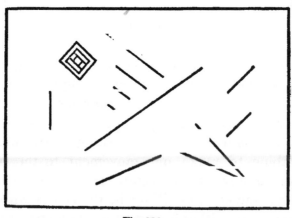

Fig. 232

In this case I have tried to balance, on the center of a symmetrical inclosure, various extensions and inclinations of tone-contrast, the movement of a convergence, and the force of a somewhat intricate and unstable symmetry.

These occult forms of Balance are not yet well understood,

and I feel considerable hesitation in speaking of them. We have certainly a great deal to learn about them. They are far better understood by the Chinese and by the Japanese than by us.

181. When any line or spot has a meaning, when there is any symbolism or representation in it, it may gain an indefinite force of attraction. This, however, is a force of attraction for the mind rather than for the eye. It affects different persons in different measures. The consideration of such attractions, suggestions, meanings, or significations does not belong to Pure Design but to Symbolism or to Representation.

TONE-RHYTHM

182. THE idea of Tone-Rhythm is expressed in every regular and perfect gradation of Tones; of values, of colors or of color-intensities, provided the eye is drawn through the gradation in one direction or in a series or sequence of directions. This happens when there is a greater tone-contrast at one end of the gradation than at the other. When the terminal contrasts are equal there is no reason why the eye should move through the gradation in any particular direction. According to our definition of Rhythm, the gradation should be marked in its stages or measures, and the stages or measures should be regular. That is certainly true, but in all regular and perfect gradations I feel that corresponding changes are taking place in corresponding measures, and I get the same feeling from such a gradation that I get from it when it is marked off in equal sections. Though the measures in regular and perfect gradations are not marked, they are, it seems to me, felt. They seem sufficiently marked by the regularity and perfection of the gradation, any irregularity or imperfection being appreciable as a break in the measure. I am inclined, therefore, to say of any regular and perfect gradation that it is rhythmical provided the direction of movement is unmistakable. The direction, as I have said, depends upon the relation of terminal contrasts. The eye is drawn toward the greater contrast, whatever that is and wherever it is. A few examples will make this clear.

				M				
Blk	LD	D	HD	M	LLt	Lt	HLt	Wt

In this case we have the gradation of the Scale of Values set on a ground-tone of the middle value. Here there are two opposed gradations with equal contrasts at the opposite ends. The result is Balance, not Rhythm.

Wt								
Blk	LD	D	HD	M	LLt	Lt	HLt	Wt

In this case we have a gradation of values beginning with White on White, no contrast at all, and reaching ultimately the contrast of Black and White. The eye is drawn through the tones of this gradation in the direction of this contrast, that is to say, from right to left. It is a clear case of Rhythm. If, instead of white, we had black, as a ground-tone, the movement of the rhythm would be in the opposite direction, — from left to right.

Wt	HLt	Lt	LLt	M	HD	D	LD	Blk
Blk	LD	D	HD	M	LLt	Lt	HLt	Wt

In this case, as in the first, we have equally great contrasts at the ends and no contrast at the middle. The result is Balance, not Rhythm.

V					
Y	YG	G	GB	B	BV

In this case, disregarding possible differences of value and color-intensities, there will be a color-rhythm proceeding from right to left. The contrast to which the eye will be drawn is the color-contrast of Yellow and Violet.

LD–V					
D–Y	HD–YG	M–G	LLt–GB	Lt–B	HLt–BV

Balance rather than Tone-Rhythm. If corresponding color and value-contrasts are not equally attractive we shall have an unequal tug-of-war between the two rhythms.

LD–V					
HLt–Y	Lt–YG	LLt–G	M–GB	HD–B	D–BV

In this case we have two rhythms, one of values and one of colors, in a Harmony of Direction. The direction of movement will be from right to left.

$HLt–Y_{\frac{1}{8}}$					
HLt–Y	$HLt–Y_{\frac{1}{8}}$	$HLt–Y_{\frac{2}{8}}$	$HLt–Y_{\frac{3}{8}}$	$HLt–Y_{\frac{4}{8}}$	$HLt–Y_{\frac{5}{8}}$

In this case we have no change of color and no change of value, but a rhythm of the intensities of one color, in one value. The movement will be from right to left. The ground-tone might be Neutral High Light, the zero-intensity of Yellow. That would not change the direction of the movement.

$LD–Y_{\frac{1}{8}}$					
HLt–Y	$Lt–Y_{\frac{1}{8}}$	$LLt–Y_{\frac{2}{8}}$	$M–Y_{\frac{3}{8}}$	$HD–Y_{\frac{4}{8}}$	$D–Y_{\frac{5}{8}}$

In this case I have indicated a combined movement of values and color-intensities. The direction of the movement will be from right to left.

The tone-rhythms which I have described are based upon the repetition at regular intervals of a certain change of value, of color or of color-intensity. We have Harmony, of course, in the repetition of equal changes, though the changes are not the same changes. The change of value from Middle to Low Light is equal to the change from Low Light to Light, though these changes are not the same changes. The Harmony is, therefore, the Harmony of equivalent contrasts which are not the same contrasts.

183. We have more or less movement in every compo-sition of tones which is unbalanced, in which the eye is not

held between equivalent attractions, either upon a vertical axis or upon a center. In all such cases, of tones unbalanced, the movement is in the direction of the greatest contrast. Unless the movement is regular and marked in its measures, as I think it is in all regular and perfect gradations, the movement is not rhythmical. We get Rhythm, however, in the repetition of the movement, whatever it is, in equal or lawfully varying measures, provided the direction of the movement remains the same or changes regularly or gradually. If the line of the movement is up-to-the-right forty-five degrees we have rhythm in the repetition of the movement at equal or lawfully varying intervals, without changes of dircetion; but we should have Rhythm, also, if the direction of the movement, in its repetitions, were changed, regularly or gradually; if, for example, the direction were changed first from up-right forty-five degrees to up-right forty degrees, then to up-right thirty-five degrees, then to up-right thirty degrees, this at equal or at lawfully varying intervals. In this way the movement of the composition repeated may be carried on and gradually developed in the movement of the series. A reference to Fig. 161, p. 94, and to Fig. 119, p. 68, will help the reader to understand these statements.

COMPOSITION

185. IT is quite impossible for me, in this discussion of terms and principles, to indicate, in any measure, the possibilities of composition, in lines and spots of paint, in tones, measures, and shapes. This is in no sense a Book of Designs. All I have undertaken to do is to give a few very simple examples and to indicate the kind of reasoning to be followed, recommending the same kind of reasoning in all cases. There are three general rules, however, which I must state.

First. Given a certain outline and certain tones, measures, and shapes to be put into it, it is the Problem of Pure Design to do the best we can, getting as many connections making unity as possible. The process is one of experimenting, observing, comparing, judging, arranging and rearranging, taking no end of time and pains to achieve Order, the utmost possible Order, if possible the Beautiful.

Second. When only an outline is given and we can put into it lines and spots of paint, — tones, measures, and shapes, — *ad libitum*, we must be sure that in the addition and multiplication of features we do not get less Order than we had in the simple outline with which we started, when it had nothing in it. As we proceed to add features we must be sure that we are not diminishing the order of the composition as a whole. If the composition as a whole is orderly, we do not want to make it less so by cutting it up and introducing additional attractions which may be disorderly and confusing. It may be harder to achieve Order with a greater number and variety of terms. We may deserve credit for overcoming this difficulty, but it is a difficulty which confronts us only when the terms are given and we have to make the best of them. When no terms are given, only a perfectly orderly outline, we should hesitate before we put anything into it. If we add anything we must be sure that it does not diminish, in the slightest degree, the order we had before, when we had nothing but the outline. The order of the whole must never be diminished.

Third. When we have an outline with certain tones, measures, and shapes in it, the question is: whether we can increase the order by adding other tones, other measures, or other shapes.

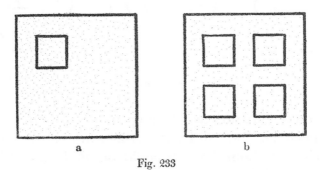

Fig. 233

Arrangement "a" is less orderly than arrangement "b," so I have acted wisely in adding the other outlines.

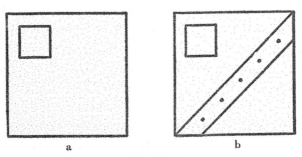

Fig. 234

sake of variety or novelty, to give a change of feeling, a new
sensation, but such motives are not the motives of Pure
Design. In Pure Design our motive is, always, to achieve
Order, in the hope that in so doing we may achieve a supreme
instance of it which will be beautiful.

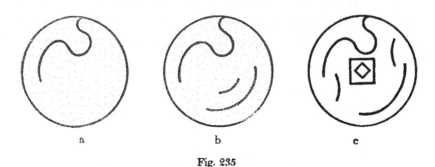

a   b   c

Fig. 235

Consider these illustrations. Arrangement "b" is more orderly
than arrangement "a," so I am justified in making the additions. The additions have brought occult balance into the
composition with Direction and Interval-Harmony. Arrangement "c" is less orderly than "b," less orderly than "a." It
has, therefore, no value for us. There is no merit in the
multiplication of features which it exhibits. The surface is
"enriched" at the expense of Direction-Harmony, Interval-
Harmony, and Shape-Harmony. There may be an approximation to an occult balance in arrangement "c," but you
cannot feel it unmistakably as you do in "b." Its value is,
therefore, less.

186. I object to the word "decoration," as commonly used
by designers, because it implies that additions are likely to be
improvements, that to multiply features, to enrich surfaces,
is worth while or desirable. The fact is, that additions are, as
a rule, to be avoided. There is no merit in the mere multiplication of features. It is a mistake. The rule of Pure Design, and
it is the rule for all Design, is simplification rather than com-
plication. As designers we ought to avoid additions, if possible.

We ought to make them only when in so doing we are able to increase the order of the whole. We make additions, indeed, to achieve the greater simplicity of Order, and for no other reason. Our object in all cases is to achieve Order, if possible a supreme instance of Order which will be beautiful. We aim at Order and hope for Beauty.

THE STUDY OF ORDER IN NATURE AND IN WORKS OF ART

187. In connection with the practice of Pure Design, as I have described it, — the composition and arrangement of lines and spots of paint; of tones, measures, and shapes: this in the modes of Harmony, Balance, and Rhythm, for the sake of Order and in the hope of Beauty, — the student should take up the study of Order in its three modes, as revealed in Nature and achieved in Works of Art.

188. The method of study should be a combination of analysis with synthetic reproduction. Taking any instance of Order, whether in Nature or in some work of Art, the first thing to do is to consider its terms, — its positions, its lines, its areas, its measure and space-relations, its tones and tone-relations, — bringing every element to separate and exact definition. The next thing to do is to note every occurrence of Harmony, of Balance, of Rhythm, — every connection making for consistency, unity, Order. In that way we shall get an exact knowledge of the case. We shall know all the facts, so far as the terms and the principles of Design are concerned. That is what I mean by analysis. By a synthetic reproduction I mean a reproduction of the effect or design, whatever it is, following the images which we have in mind as the result of our analysis. The reproduction should be made without reference to the effect or design which has been analyzed. There should be no direct imitation, no copying. We must not depend so much upon the memory as upon the imagination. Having reproduced the effect or design in this way, following the suggestions of the imagination, the reproduction should be brought into comparison with the effect or design reproduced and the differences noted. Differences should be carefully

observed and the previous analysis should be reviewed and reconsidered. When this is done another attempt at reproduction should be made. This process should be repeated until the effect or design is thoroughly understood and imaginatively grasped. The evidence of understanding and comprehension will be seen in the reproduction which is made, which ought to have an essential but not a literal correspondence with the original. Analysis should precede; synthesis should follow.

I hope, in another book or books, to be published later, to give some examples of Order in natural objects or effects, also examples of Order in Works of Art, with a careful analysis of each one, showing how the points, lines, and areas, the measure and the space-relations, the tones and tone-relations come together in the forms of Harmony, Balance, and Rhythm, in the modes of Order, in instances of Beauty. In the mean time, as the methods of analytic study and of synthetic practice are clearly indicated in the preceding pages, the student who has taken pains to understand what he has read will find himself well prepared for the work. He can take up the study of Order in Nature and of Design in Works of Art without further assistance.

CONCLUSION

189. IT does not follow, even when our minds, in consequence of the study and the practice which I have described, are richly stored with the terms and the motives of Design, that we shall produce anything important or remarkable. Important work comes only from important people. What we accomplish, at best, is merely the measure and expression of our own personalities. Nevertheless, though we may not be able to produce anything important, it is something to appreciate and enjoy what is achieved by others. If our studies and our work bring us to the point of visual discrimination, to æsthetic appreciation and enjoyment, and no farther, we are distinguished among men. The rarest thing in the world is creative genius, the faculty which creates great works. Next to that comes the faculty of appreciation. That, too, is rare. We must not believe that appreciation is easy. It is true that the recognition of Order is instinctive and spontaneous, but untrained people recognize it only in a few simple and obvious forms. Order in its higher forms — the order of a great number and variety of terms and of different principles in combination — lies altogether beyond the appreciation of untrained people. It is only as we are trained, exercised, and practiced in the use of terms and in following principles that we rise to the appreciation of great achievements. The sense of order, which we all have, in a measure, needs to be exercised and developed. The spontaneity of undeveloped faculty does not count for much. It carries us only a little way. Let no one believe that without study and practice in Design he can recognize and appreciate what is best in Design.

Appreciation and enjoyment are the rewards of hard thinking with hard work. In order to appreciate the masterpiece we must have some knowledge of the terms which the artist has used and the principles which he has followed. We know the terms only when we have ourselves used them, and the principles when we have tried to follow them. The reason why the appreciation of excellence in speech and in writing is so widespread is due to the fact that we all speak and write, constantly, and try, so many of us, to speak and write well. The reason why there is so little appreciation of excellence in other forms of art is due to the fact that the terms are not in general use and the principles are not understood, as they should be, in the light of personal experience and effort. It is for this reason that I am anxious to see the teaching and practice of Design introduced into the schools, public and private, everywhere, and into our colleges as well as our schools. I have no idea that many able designers will be produced, but what I expect, as a result of this teaching, is a more general understanding of Design, more interest in it, and more appreciation and enjoyment of its achievements. Among the many who will appreciate and enjoy will be found the few who will create and produce.

The purpose of what is called art-teaching should be the production, not of objects, but of faculties, — the faculties which being exercised will produce objects of Art, naturally, inevitably. Instead of trying to teach people to produce Art, which is absurd and impossible, we must give them a training which will induce visual sensitiveness with æsthetic discrimination, an interest in the tones, measures, and shapes of things, the perception and appreciation of Order, the sense of Beauty. In these faculties we have the causes of Art. Inducing the causes, Art will follow as a matter of course. In exercising and developing the faculties which I have named, which naturally and inevitably produce Art, we are doing all that can be done by teaching. There is no better training for the visual and æsthetic faculties than is found in the practice of Pure Design, inducing, as it does, discrimination in tones, measures, and shapes, and the appreciation of what is orderly and beautiful. The result of the practice will be a wide spread of visual and æsthetic faculty which will have, as its natural and inevitable result, the appreciation and the production of Works of Art.

Our object, then, in the study and practice of Pure Design is, not so much the production of Works of Art, as it is to induce in ourselves the art-loving and art-producing faculties. With these faculties we shall be able to discover Order and Beauty everywhere, and life will be happier and better worth living, whether we produce Works of Art, ourselves, or not. We shall have an impulse which will lead us to produce Works of Art if we can. At the same time we shall have the judgment which will tell us whether what we have done is or is not beautiful.

PARAGRAPH INDEX

PARAGRAPH INDEX

1, p. 1. The Meaning of Design.

2, p. 1. The Order of Harmony.

3, p. 1. The Order of Balance.

4, p. 2. The Order of Rhythm.

5, p. 2. Relations of Harmony, Balance, and Rhythm.

6, p. 4. Beauty a supreme instance of Order.

7, p. 4. The Arts as different modes of Expression.

8, p. 5. Drawing and Painting.

9, p. 5. Two modes of Drawing and Painting.

10, p. 5. Pure Design.

11, p. 6. Applied Design.

12, p. 7. Representation.

13, p. 7. Representation in Forms of Design.

14, p. 9. The Definition of Positions.

15, p. 9. The Relation of Directions and Distances.

16, p. 10. Directions defined.

17, p. 11. Distances defined.

18, p. 11. Positions determined by Triangulations.

19, p. 11. Intervals.

20, p. 12. Scale in Relations of Position.

21, p. 12. Harmony of Positions.

22, p. 12. Harmony of Directions.

23, p. 13. Harmony of Distances.

24, p. 14. Harmony of Intervals.

25, p. 16. Intervals in any series of Positions.

26, p. 17. Positions and their possibilities.

27, p. 17. Balance of opposite Directions.

28, p. 17. Balance of Distances in opposite Directions.

29, p. 18. Balance of Directions not opposite.

30, p. 18. Balance of Distances in Directions not opposite.

31, p. 19. Positions in Balance.

32, p. 19. Stable equilibrium of vertical and horizontal directions.

33, p. 20. Symmetry defined.

34, p. 21. The central axis should predominate in symmetrical Balances.

35, p. 22. Balance in Relations of Position, when inverted.

36, p. 22 Finding the center of equilibrium in unbalanced relations of position Indication of centers by symmetrical inclosures.

37, p. 24. Tendency of symmetrical inclosures, when sufficiently attractive, to prevent movement.

38, p. 25. How unstable equilibrium suggests movement.

39, p. 26. Rhythmic movement in a gradual increase in the number of attractions through a series of visual angles.

40, p. 27. The possibilities of rhythmic movement in relations of position.

41, p. 27. Balanced attractions at equal intervals give no movement, consequently no Rhythm.

42, p. 28. The gradual increase of attractions in a series of visual angles, as produced by gradual changes of scale, causes rhythmic movement.

43, p. 28. How unbalanced groups of positions being repeated at equal intervals produce rhythmic movement.

44, p. 29. Rhythmic movements produced by the repetition of unbalanced relations of position and by a gradual diminution of scale.

45, p. 30. Rhythmic movements produced by the repetition of a balanced relation of positions with a gradual diminution of intervals, causing a gradual increase of attractions through a series of visual angles. | 67, 68, 69, 70,

46, p. 30. Rhythmic movements produced by the repetition of a balanced relation of positions with diminution of intervals and of scale. | 71, 72, 73,

47, p. 31. Rhythmic movements produced by the repetition of an unbalanced relation of positions with a crowding due to gradual diminution of intervals. | 74, 75,

48, p. 31. Rhythmic movements produced by the repetition of an unbalanced relation of positions with a diminution of measure in the intervals and of scale in the groups. The combination of two or more rhythms. | 76, 77,

49, p. 32. The combination of two or more rhythms. | 78,

50, p. 32. Relations of position in different attitudes. | 79,

51, p. 33. Principal Attitudes.

52, p. 34. Harmony in Attitudes. | 80,

53, p. 35. Harmony in the repetition of any relation of attitudes.

54, p. 35. Balance in Attitudes.

55, p. 36. Rhythm in Attitudes. | 81,

56, p. 37. The Line.

57, p. 37. Changes of Direction in a line. Angles. | 82,

58, p. 38. Gradual changes of Direction in a line. Curves. | 83,

59, p. 41. Curves regarded as compositions of circular arcs. | 84,

60, p. 42. Differences of scale in lines.

61, p. 42. Differences of attractive force in lines. | 85,

62, p. 44. Harmony of Direction in lines. | 86,

63, p. 44. Harmony of Angles in lines.

64, p. 45. Harmony in Legs of Angles. | 87,

65, p. 45. Harmony in Curvatures. | 88,

66, p. 46. Harmony in Arcs when they have the same radius. | 89,

f Lines.	115, p. 112. Harmony, Balance, and Rhythm in the Attitudes of Outlines.
f Lines.	
ines.	116, p. 112. The Composition of Outlines.
›mposi-	
ˈ ratios	117, p. 124. The purpose of designing to induce the sense of Beauty which is the cause of all that is fine in Design.
r Har-	
es.	118, p. 125. Areas.
›osition	119, .p. 125. Linear Areas.
	120, p. 125. Changes of width-measure in Linear Progressions.
without	
	121, p. 129. Areas defined by outlines, and also by tone-contrasts.
without	
	122, p. 131. The Composition of Areas as defined by tone-contrasts.
librium	
alances	123, p. 131. Difference between drawing and painting, if there is any.
›y sym-	
	124, p. 131. Definition of the word Tone.
ıs.	125, p. 132. Tone-Analysis.
ı the	126, p. 132. The study of Tones and Tone-Relations.
various	127, p. 133. Pigment-Materials.
move-	128, p. 133. The Scale of Neutral Values.
	129, p. 134. Contrasts of the Scale of Values.
ily in-	
e.	130, p. 135. Definition of Value-Relations.
ˈarious	
	131, p. 136. Scales of Colors in Different Values.
and	132, p. 137. Definition of the terms used to describe different Colors.
of an	133, p. 138. Color-Intensities found in different values.
›imen-	134, p. 139. Value-Relation of different Colors shown in the Spectrum.
ıse of	
	135, p. 139. The Spectrum a sequence not a circuit; a circuit in pigments only.
ɾence.	
›nver-	136, p. 140. The Complementaries.
ɑ in	137, p. 140. A General Classification of Tones as to Value, Color, Color-Intensity, and Color-Neutralization.
hyth-	
ım in	
. . ..	138, p. 141. The distinction between

139, p. 141. Definition of particular tones.

140, p. 141. Theoretical character of our classification of tones. 160, p.

141, p. 142. Definition of particular tone-relations.

142, p. 143. Sequences of Values and Colors.

143, p. 143. The Sequence of Neutral Values. 161, p.

144, p. 144. Vertical Sequences.

145, p. 144. Horizontal Sequences. 162, p.

146, p. 144. Diagonal Sequences. 163, p.

147, p. 145. Diagonal Sequences of the Right and Left Modes.

148, p. 146. Different Intervals in Diagonal Sequences. 164, p. 165, p.

149, p. 146. Peculiar value of the Diagonal Sequence of Colors at the interval of the Fifth. The four Triads. 166, p. 167, p.

150, p. 147. Sequences in which a certain relation of intervals is repeated. 168, p.

151, p. 147. The combination of two or more Vertical Sequences. 169, p.

152, p. 148. The combination of two or more Horizontal Sequences.

153, p. 149. The Combination of Diagonal Sequences of the same and different modes. 170, p.

154, p. 151. Alternations in Vertical Sequences. 171, p.

155, p. 151. Alternations in Horizontal Sequences.

156, p. 151. Alternations of different value-intervals in color-sequences of equal intervals. 172, p. 173, p.

157, p. 153. Alternations of different color-intervals in value-sequences of equal intervals. Particular Sequences recommended. 174, p. 175, p.

158, p. 153. Possibility of extending the classification of values and colors to a scale of seventeen values, including Black and White. 176, p. 177, p.

159, p. 154. The method of using the Sequences described. Possible 178, p.

179, p. 178. Further considerations on the same subject.
180, p. 178. Further considerations on the same subject.
181, p. 181. The effect of Representations in Tone-Balances.
182, p. 182. Tone-Rhythm.
183, p. 184. Attitudes in Tone-Rhythms.
184, p. 185. Inversions in Tone-Rhythms.
185, p. 186. Composition of tones, mea-sures, and shapes. Three general rules.
186, p. 188. Design and " Decoration."
187, p. 190. The study of Order in Nature and in Works of Art.
188, p. 190. Method of study by Analysis with Synthetic Performance.
189, p. 192. Conclusion. The practice of Pure Design. Its purpose and end.

ND - #0120 - 070223 - C0 - 229/152/12 - PB - 9781440088919 - Gloss Lamination